Letters from Cleo and Tyrone

Letters from Cleo and Tyrone

A Feline Perspective on Love, Life, and Litter

Discovered and Compiled by
L. VIRGINIA BROWNE AND LINDA HAMNER

Illustrated by STEVE FELDMAN

St. Martin's Griffin New York

Illustrations by Steve Feldman. Used by permission.

Book design by Michelle McMillian

www.stmartins.com

Library of Congress Cataloging-in-Publication Data
Browne, L. Virginia.
    Letters from Cleo and Tyrone : a feline perspective on love, life, and litter
/ discovered and compiled by L. Virginia Browne and Linda Hamner ;
illustrated by Steve Feldman. — 1st ed.
        p. cm.
    ISBN 0-312-26706-1
    1. Cats—Fiction. 2. Women cat owners—Fiction. 3. Human-animal
relationships—Fiction. I. Hamner, Linda. II. Feldman, Steve. III. Title.
PS3552.R747 L4 2000
813'.6—dc21   00-040515

10 9 8 7 6 5 4 3 2

For Marisa and Taylor, David and Maggie, Colette and Mac, my mother, Raymonde, and for my father, Clifford Conklin Browne, the finest human being I have ever known

—LVB

For Gary, Brent, and Karen, grandkids Nathan, Sarah, Alex, and my father, Gilbert Dixon Gadberry, who taught me the joy of words—cat lovers all!

—LH

Excuse us, but who are the TRUE authors here?

For Hardenburg, Bismarck, Miss Marple, Chester, and Lucy, who, although of the canine persuasion, were very *amusant* and all-around good eggs.

And for Charles and Remy, role models extraordinaire; everything feline we learned from them.

We miss them all.

—Cleo and Tyrone

Letters from Cleo and Tyrone

PREFACE

To: LVB447@msn.com (L. Virginia Browne)
From: LindaHamner@att.net
Subject: Cleo and Tyrone

Dear Virginia,

Something remarkable has happened. Remarkable and amazing. And maybe a little scary, too.

While straightening out the cat toy box—you know the one, the red box in the hall filled with expensive cat toys that neither Cleo, Honey, nor Stealth ever plays with?—I found several computer diskettes buried at the very bottom. I was puzzled, but then I may well have dropped them on my way from the computer room to the den. Highly unlikely, I concede, but possible.

I put one of the diskettes into the computer and what came up on the screen was absolute gibberish. After checking the others, they were all the same: nonsense letters and characters. At least, that's what I assumed it was. Upon closer examination, I noticed a certain pattern, a recurrence of symbols that caused me to suspect it might be some alien language. Hmmm-mm . . .

So I then took the suspect set of diskettes to Professor Manfred "Mannie" Katz of the UCLA Linguistics Department. After several weeks of analysis, Dr. Katz announced a breakthrough: he thought, at first, it was the more common Catçais; upon further examination, however, he realized it was Felinese. He explained that Felinese is to Catçais what London-area English is to Outback Australian. He was, to say the least, impressed.

Conclusion: our resident felines, my Cleo and your Tyrone, have been communicating with each other via e-mail. And here I'd assumed the kibble in the hard drive and the white fur on the keyboard were the result of my poor housekeeping. Well, that, too.

I'm enclosing a copy of the translation. I don't know if I'm overreacting, perhaps reading something into their missives that really isn't there, but I'm nervous. Who knows what harebrained scheme the diabolical duo might be planning next?

What do you think?

Love,

Linda

Diskette I

To: TyroneTheGreat@aol.com
From: CleoTheDivine@att.net
Subject: Dangerous Liaisons

Dearest Tyrone,

I just wanted to thank you for allowing Honey, Stealth, and me to stay with you this Thanksgiving while our mommy and daddy were away God-knows-where on vacation. While they were off après-skiing in Gstaad or snorkeling off Arugula, they just dumped us in our lousy carriers on your doorstep without so much as an introduction. We are all so grateful that especially you, Tyrone, and LizzieBeth treated us with such kindness and generosity—always willing to share that patch of sun on top of the kitty condo, letting us play with your catnip toys (*whee!*) and sharing your food with us. I hope you enjoy the catnip-filled chocolate fish and birds I sent. I know it appears that five of them are missing, but for some reason when I ordered them on-line, that's how they arrived. Go figure. Or the dog ate them. Yes, that's it. The Big Old Stupid Dog ate them.

Don't you think Honey, who they claim is my twin, is downright peculiar? She never wants to knead my mommy's stomach, and get this, she doesn't even want to sit in the middle of her crossword puzzle or book. And I've never once seen her sit on Mommy's dinner plate. Or her head. It just isn't normal.

And what can you say about Stealth? Well, the cat's a thug. What did my mommy expect when she adopted him? He had been living on the streets for years and had developed no social skills whatsoever. That cat wouldn't know Lalique from a lollipop. And his physique! That fireplug of a body on top of those short Lincoln Log legs. When he tries to swish his short, scrawny tail imperiously—as cats are supposed to do—he just looks ridiculous. I'm embarrassed for him. I really am.

Now, far be it from me to say anything negative about the other feline in your house, but I do worry that LizzieBeth might not always have your best interests at heart. Just be careful, dear Tyrone. That's all I'm suggesting. I wouldn't put it past her to be a tattletail. Unfortunately, I know this from personal experience. One morning I was trying to help your mommy by straightening the pet-snack drawer. LizzieBeth sauntered in, took one look at me, and she high-tailed it out of there like her pathetic little tail was on fire. I peeked into the living room and saw she was whispering something into your mommy's ear. The next thing I knew I was in trouble.

That seems to be the story of my life—always being unjustly accused. Whenever anything goes wrong at my house, it's somehow my fault. Just because I happen to be on top of the refrigerator and the apples suddenly fall to the floor, it's automatically my fault. Has Mommy never heard of Newton? Of gravity? Wasn't that the whole theory of apples anyway?

And I couldn't help but notice, Tyrone, that LizzieBeth has quite a little crush on you. She follows you everywhere and looks at you with those insipid goo-goo eyes. It's very obvious how she feels. Although I noticed she wasn't sporting a solitaire on her left paw, I really don't know how you feel about her. Are you two an item? I'm blushing as I tell you I have more than a passing interest in the response to my question.

I must admit, dearest Tyrone, when I walked into your living room and saw you hanging there, seemingly suspended in midair, as you scaled that wall hanging, you took my breath away. Your beautiful, muscular sculpted body . . . *magnifique!* I knew instantly you were my soulmate. It goes without saying, of course, you feel exactly the same way about me, *n'est-ce pas?*

Your dog, Lucy, is a lot easier to deal with than that lug I've got at my house. At least Lucy is a manageable size. My dog, Chester, is the size of a moose and has the IQ of a dessert of the same name. I must be fair, however; dogs can provide a diversion when one is truly bored. When the dog is really sound asleep, I like to rub up against his big old nose. Back and forth I go. Rub, rub, rub. Eventually, he awakens, sneezing his big old head off. I find that *amusant.* Also, as he walks by, I like to take a swat at him. For no particular reason. Just because it's fun.

Sacre bleu! There's Mommy bellowing at me. "Cle-o. Cle-o!!" Lordy, is that woman's voice annoying or what! She sounds exactly like a demented, beached humpback whale. Time for *moi* to make myself very tiny and disappear until she gets those pesky hormones under control.

And I had so much more to discuss with you. Dearest Tyrone, I have reason to believe your very life might be in danger. Oh God, thar she blows again! "Clee-o!!!" Watch your back. And front. I'll explain later.

Warmest regards,

Cleo

To: CleoTheDivine@att.net
From: TyroneTheGreat@aol.com
Subject: Dismissing Danger and Dogs

Dear Cleo,

Now that Thanksgiving is gone and the Christmas holidays are upon us, I have decided to take a break from composing my gift list (what I want, of course, not what I intend to give) and respond to your plaintive missive of yesterday. I had no idea what a void would exist once you and your sister, Honey (and Stealth, of course) left to go back to your own home. I know you miss me. In fact, I'll bet anything you're pining for me right now. Perhaps even crying. Ah, you female felines are so emotional. My advice, *ma petite amie?* Focus instead on the upcoming holidays. Who knows? Maybe my mommy will go away and I'll be sent to spend the vacation with you and your siblings. It could happen.

But, that dealt with, Cleo, sweetie, my life might be in danger? My, but you do have a flair for the dramatic. My life might be in danger. . . .

I scoff at danger. I entice danger. I laugh at danger. Ha-ha-ha. Imagine, if you will, my paws on my hips and a dagger in my mouth. Ha-ha-ha. Yes, much better.

Imagine, if you will,
my paws on my hips and a
dagger in my mouth.

I am the mighty Tyrone, afraid of nothing. Except maybe an empty food dish. If I could only figure out a way to get those cans open . . .

Anyway, on to the crisis du jour. Boy, oh, boy, have I had it. I tell you, meow almighty, I have had it.

You remember Lucy the Dog? Of course you do. She's that spoiled brat prima donna princess who absolutely insists on eating some of my leftover Thanksgiving turkey. So who's the turkey? Me. My mommy put out some turkey—though mostly dark meat when she knows I prefer white—such a bitch—but I digress. . . .

Truth be told, I wasn't hungry at that exact moment. I know some might remark that I jumped up and down on Mommy as soon as the sun came up, insisting on having my dish filled, but once she was up, I guess I just wasn't hungry anymore. So call the police. Then Mommy let Lucy out into the backyard, cleaned up our dishes, cleaned out the water dishes and replaced the water with fresh water (filtered, thank you very much; the chlorine in the water around here is simply overwhelming to the point it absolutely overpowers the tantalizing aroma of a good, freshly killed mouse or lizard, but again I digress), changed the eating rug, dished dry food into the dry bowl, then opened the cans of food and dished them out. Then she took a turkey thigh out of the food cooler-keeper that we have to stay out of for fear of being trapped with lots to eat but not a lot of air to breathe, cut it up, put it on plates for us, set those plates on the eating rug, and then let the dog back in. I was just exhausted from watching her. And not hungry anymore. Can you blame me? I swear . . .

Fatigued, I went onto Mommy's bed, upon which she had just put fresh sheets last night (will she never learn?) and nestled into a fresh pile of pillows on the left side to sleep. And Lucy ate my turkey. Now, you probably can't imagine it could get any worse, could you? Well, pay attention, please. When I awoke a few hours later, I decided I needed a change of scenery. The window seats were in place and the windows widely open, so I delicately leapt onto the cream-colored sheepskin seat, nestled down into the soft fur, the wind blowing gently onto me, the sun shining, and . . . Wait a minute! Wind blowing *what* onto me? Oh, my God . . .

You guessed it. The turkey didn't exactly agree with the doggy princess, and when taking a stroll in the great outdoors, she decided to attend to her distress—right under my window!! I sniffed the air: *dégoûtante.* I opened one eye and lifted my head carefully: it was right under my window. Wafting up through the window. I hate dogs.

Something had to be done, and I was just the Feisty Feline to do it. I am strong, I am big, I am Tyrone the Mighty!

But, first, about that danger thing. What, exactly, do you mean? Not that I'm scared, mind you. But one must remain informed if one is to be prepared. Just in case. Not that I'm worried. Or even too interested. Yawn . . .

But could you be a little more specific, *mon petit fleur?*
Ever yours in readiness and waiting,
Tyrone the Terrific

TO: TyroneTheGreat@aol.com
FROM: CleoTheDivine@att.net
SUBJECT: Fractured Femurs and Fantasies

My Dearest Tyrone,

I know you are the bravest, strongest, most valiant feline on the planet. Nobody does feats of derring-do like you do derring-do, dear. Which reminds me—you also have the most adorable derrière. But I fear I'm getting off track. As hard as it is to accept, you must believe me when I tell you that you have put way too much trust in your mommy. Yes, I agree she gets high marks for providing superior chow. Additional bonus points for very clean litter and lots of comfy pillows and nifty hiding places. I know you see her as a combination of Mother Teresa, Jane Goodall, and Betty White. I, on the other hand, see her as a combo of Norman Bates, Hannibal Lecter, and Cruella De Vil. Why, you ask, am I so harsh on your mommy? I haven't seen you since my terrible accident, but I've had a great deal of time to reflect on that horrible disaster. Alas, I'm afraid I can come to no other conclusion than it was your very own mommy who was responsible for my near demise.

Now as I remember the incident—and I am known for my excellent memory—I was just strolling from bookcase to bookcase when suddenly I found myself on the floor, my long, shapely leg smashed to smithereens. On top of my crushed body a stereo speaker came to rest. Your mommy shrieked in horror. To be honest, I think she was more upset with her busted speaker than she was with broken *moi*.

Your mommy claims I accidentally tripped. Or that my leg got tangled in the stereo cord or some such nonsense. Oh, puhleez. Remember, I'm a model. I make my living slinking up and down catwalks. Did you ever hear of me once going splat off the side of the runway? I think not. No, I fear it was far more sinister. I was deliberately pushed, pulled, or tripped. And your mommy was standing right there when the ugly incident occurred. Suddenly, there I was on the floor, writhing in indescribable pain, my leg broken. I think she had a guilty conscience or something because she sure was quick to whisk me up into her arms and hurl me into one of those dreadful carriers and transport me to that torture chamber laughingly called the "emergency animal hospital."

There they put my delicate little paw in a cast. It made it impossible to walk on four legs as God—and I—had intended. I had to hobble about on three legs, that right front leg held stiffly in front of me at a one-hundred-and-twenty-degree angle from the ground. I looked like the poster cat for Felines for Hitler, and I felt at any moment I might break into a chorus of "Tomorrow Belongs to Us" from *Cataret*. Oh, Tyrone, I'm just so relieved you didn't have to see me like that. I fear it would have broken your heart.

And if that weren't bad enough, they then put this contraption

I'm not exaggerating when I tell you three dogs, two cats, a pot-bellied pig, and a ferret guffawed at me when I hobbled through.

around my neck. I don't know what it's called, but its sole function is clearly feline abuse. Imagine, if you will, if someone had crammed a megaphone over my head, the skinny end around my neck, the big end extending way beyond my head. If you had called me, "Hey, Funnel Head," it would, alas, have been an accurate epithet.

Finally my mommy—who I'm sure belongs to the same coven

as your mommy—came to pick me up. Although I might add, she sure took her sweet time getting there. You know what she did when she saw me? When I think about it, I still choke up. She . . . She . . . laughed! Does she really think it's *amusant* that my modeling days are over? That I might never work again as a paw model? Oh, cruelty, thy name is Mommy.

Did they let me make a discreet exit through the back door? *Mais non!* Mommy marched me right through the waiting room. I'm not exaggerating when I tell you three dogs, two cats, a pot-bellied pig, and a ferret guffawed at me when I hobbled through. And do you have any idea how loud a group guffaw sounds when you're wearing a megaphone over your head?

Mommy finally took the megaphone off this morning. I don't think she did it out of compassion for me. I think maybe she got tired of picking up the papers my megaphone "accidentally" knocked off the table. The final coup de grâce might have been the Baccarat dog that went careening off the coffee table and crashing onto the floor. *Ooops!*

I sure hope the cast comes off soon. The holiday season is just around the corner, and I was planning on knitting sweaters for one and all. I designed a special one for you, my dearest Tyrone. Very *GQ*. But alas, I don't know if it's possible to knit with only one paw.

I would like to extend an invitation to you and LizzieBeth (and Lucy, if you must) to spend some time with us during the holidays. Perhaps your mommy is going on a long, long trip? Just think of the fun we could have: baking those yummy tuna Santa Claws cookies, playing Christmas ornament soccer, and stringing Christmas lights on the dog. I love that part.

Extend my good wishes to your little family. And be careful—

be very careful—when you're strolling on the bookcases. Evil spirits (she knows who she is!) lurk there, just waiting to hurl you into the abyss.

Lighting a candle for your safety,

Cleo

To: CleoTheDivine@att.net
FROM: TyroneTheGreat@aol.com
SUBJECT: Feline Rule #6

Dear Cleo,

Your paw was really broken? Gosh, and here I thought all the screaming and meowing you did that fateful night was for dramatic effect. Go figure.

But in my mommy's defense, I really don't think she hurled you from the top of that ominous bookcase. Really, I don't. She has her faults, Lord knows, but let's face it: she just isn't tall enough to even REACH the top of the bookcase, much less hurl you down from it. No, I suspect you might consider the possibility that the stereo speaker wires themselves had it in for you. I've heard such grudges can be held, you know. Not against me, of course, since any and all such inanimate objects step from my path out of both fear and respect, but you, being a girl and all, might have some problems. Next time, just come to me and I'll handle it. Unless, of course, the source of your vexation is, well, too vexing.

Now, I know you didn't ask, but I feel compelled to continue my tale of Tyrone versus Lucy the Dog. When we last left our story, a malodorous scent was wafting up and through the window where I sat innocently upon my perch. And what did I do?

I quickly jumped onto the nightstand and from there onto the bed. Where is Mommy? I must tell her of this incredible breach of etiquette, of this unbearable transgression by that fuzzy creature. But she's not there. Wait, it's not dark. Mommy is only here on the bed when it's dark. Or when she eats too much and takes what she quaintly refers to as a "catnap" to sleep it off.

And, by the by, why is it called a "catnap"? Is what people folk do even vaguely akin to a catnap? Do they first scratch around in a litter box, relieve themselves, and then—depending on whether they are top cat—examine their handiwork and cover it or not? I don't think so. Do they then stretch out on the floor and then sit up, raise their back leg straight up in the air and lick their ass with their tongues? If they do, I've never seen it. Do they then find a friendly feline, usually smaller than themselves, to give a face washing? I seem to recall some humans using items referred to as soap and a washcloth. Not the same thing at all.

But back to catnaps: now, while I have no objection to grabbing a few z's in a nicely laid out king-size bed, no self-respecting feline would so restrict him- or herself. Not when so many other perfectly acceptable sleeping spots exist: the top of the refrigerator; on the television (preferably on, as it's warmer that way); behind the toilet (in hot weather only, thank you very much); on new furniture, especially if it is in a color distinctly opposite to yours, such as a white cat on a black couch, or vice versa, and if it's shedding season; on one of the beams in the living room ceiling; in the bathtub; in a closet, especially if there are lots of soft things on the floor like blankets or stuff; or on the top of very high furniture or bookcases, especially if you can hide out of sight and drive your mommy into an absolute frenzy searching for you. And please recall Basic Feline Rule #6: never—but never—come when your name is called. In fact, the moment you hear your name, compress your body into the size of an olive, become as still and invisible as a salesperson in Bloomingdales, and go back to sleep. It'll make the mommies crazy, and hence, they'll love you all the more.

But to continue with catnaps: come on, now, most humans have never slept in any of the above-mentioned places—in fact, they've never even considered sleeping in any of those places. And yet they call themselves "catnap takers." Poppycock. And when they sleep, do they either curl into a tight ball, head tucked neatly into their own crotches, or do they let themselves drop into a totally casual position possible only if they have not a single bone in their body? I didn't think so. Case closed.

But where is Mommy? TV room? No, though the set is on. Ah, kitchen. Wow, look at this: lots of dishes and they're all empty. So is the dry kibble dish, disgusting as that stuff is. And, of course, all that great turkey is gone. That's what started this trek in the first place. What to do, what to do, what to do . . .

So I howled. I sat down in the middle of the rug in the kitchen—no need to tucker myself out over this—lifted my head, opened my mouth, and let out the most plaintive cry of which I was capable. I must admit that I have refined a cry that would bring ghosts from the garret to determine the cause. But wait— no one has come. I have not managed to evoke a single re- sponse. When I thought about it, the place was pretty quiet. Even when Mommy doesn't come, I can usually count on LizzieBeth to show up. I know, I know: she says I'm a spoiled brat, but that's

In fact, the moment you hear your name, compress your body to the size of an olive...

only because, as you so perceptively noticed and mentioned, she has a crush on me. She's always following me around and stuff. Girls . . .

Ah, the living room. I bounded out of the kitchen, down the hall, and into the dining room. I jumped up onto the table and surveyed the living room and saw—nothing. There wasn't a feline or canine in sight. I lifted my head and sniffed. Nothing. I opened my mouth to draw more odors into my scent glands and then I smelled it: my family. But where were they?

I sauntered into the entryway and suddenly realized the danger all too evident with the unexpected and self-defining presence of the dreaded carrier. There was only one in evidence. And then I heard it: the meowing of a cat. I leapt atop the carrier and looked out the glass in the front door. And the family truck, a satanic vehicle with its yawning maw open and visible, was parked with its back to the front door, and there in the back were two carriers. In one, the big one, was Lucy the Dog. And in the other, clearly visible, was LizzieBeth. Frantic, she was crying and then, upon seeing me, began calling my name.

Sudden realization struck. Oh my gosh, oh my gosh, they're all going somewhere and they forgot me! Oh, meow, meow, meow! What will I do? What can I do? And then, from behind me, came that noise. It was footsteps, my mommy's footsteps. She smiled and picked me up and hugged me. She said she'd been looking all over for me, and that she'd been so worried, and that we were going to have to go to the vet for our exams. (Yeah, right, "our.") I licked her face. She likes that. And I wrapped my paws around her wrist. But only because she likes that, too, and not because I was so happy to see her and relieved that she hadn't forgotten me. I'm not a softie, after all, and I really wasn't scared, anyway. And then I didn't fuss much at all when she put me in my carrier and took me out to the car. I knew that when we came home, there'd be lots of food and hugs, and everybody would be together and I would have plenty of time to talk to Mommy about Lucy the Dog—and why I really think it would be in her best interest if she was sent to a farm to live. . . .

So, if you know of any good farms, please let me know. And until then, just send air freshener.

Much love to you and the guys,

Tyrone the Terrible

To: TyroneTheGreat@aol.com
From: CleoTheDivine@att.net
Subject: Weedwacker Warning

My Dearest Tyrone,

Please forgive my fox paw for not inquiring how your story about Lucy the Dog concluded. I felt quite certain, if your dog is anything like mine, it would be fairly disgusting. No matter how fancy their house, no matter how long and impressive their pedigree, dogs still drink out of the toilet. That pretty much says it all, doesn't it?

I'm sure you will understand my lapse in etiquette when I tell you I have been obsessed with your safety. I was so disturbed, I wasn't even getting twenty hours of sleep a day, and I had virtually stopped eating. Mommy asked me if I were trying out for a role on *Ally McBeal,* whatever that means. Finally, in an effort to get me to eat, she fixed my favorite—that old standby, tuna-neck stew. You must understand, I ate only to keep my strength up in case you needed me, Tyrone.

Do you really think your mommy wasn't responsible for my near-fatal accident? Do you really think it could have been an inanimate object with a grudge? You know, now that I think of it, when I was a young slip of a thing, I had a run-in with a deranged Weedwacker. A very ugly incident indeed. And I seem to recall seeing a Weedwacker in your mommy's closet. That must have been it. A Weedwacker with an attitude—and a very good memory—tried to do me in.

Well, I guess I owe your mommy an apology. But I think anyone can see why she topped my list of suspects. After all, she *was* standing right next to the bookcase. . . . And why didn't she do anything to thwart the wicked Weedwacker?

But alas, I have bigger fish to fry. (Actually, I have no fish to fry, but everyone always says that. Whatever.) All I know is I am so upset I can hardly breathe. I need the comfort and support only you, sweet Tyrone, can provide. It's just so unfair. So cruel.

Last night, my mommy wanted that wretched Stealth inside. She said it was too cold for man or beast outside. Personally, the temperature felt very agreeable to me. I looked at the thermostat, and it was a perfectly acceptable seventy-two degrees. Finally the dreaded alley cat (I can feel my delicate mauve nose crinkling at the very sound of the mention of that variety of cat) showed up. He did a quick survey of MY dish and the dog's (who cares about that?). After a soupçon of catnip, Stealth jumped up on my mommy, who was once again lying on the couch. (Sometimes I get confused and can't tell the difference between the couch and my mommy. They both have arms and legs and a long horizontal place in the middle. Oh, I remember now. My mommy answers the phone; the sofa doesn't.)

You know, it really upset me. As if he owned her or something. Just who does this striped interloper think he is, anyway? While he got all nice and cozy on Mommy's lap, I scampered around to the back of the sofa and jumped up. I was just trying to be close to Mommy. She tells me all the time she likes me to stay close so she can keep her eye on me. Yes, she loves me that much. I'm sure your mommy says exactly the same thing to you. Anyway, so what does the stupid striped number do? When he sees me leaping gracefully onto the couch, he also does a leap (very poor form, I might add—I wouldn't have given him more than a 4.2, tops). During the execution of this awkward, graceless jump, he managed to scratch my poor mommy to shreds. It just killed me seeing my beloved mommy's tummy and legs so mutilated. I know I'll have nightmares about it forever.

Now this is the really crazy part. I personally would have banished that miscreant from the house FOREVER. But my mommy blamed me! Can you believe it? Do I have blood on my paws? I think not. Somehow I'm being blamed for the egregious act.

Could my mommy really think I was capable of such an act of overt violence? Apparently so. I was devastated, I can tell you. Fortunately, Honey understood my pain and managed to harass Stealth sufficiently that he insisted on being let out. Honey then called the American Feline Legal Union (AFLU) on by behalf.

If nothing else, Mommy owes me a heartfelt apology. I'm not litigious by nature, but I think anyone would agree that I am the aggrieved party here. Because I love my mommy so—in spite of her lack of trust—I might be willing to settle out of court for a case of tuna (albacore naturally, but of course that goes without saying, *n'est-ce pas?*).

Ty, thank you for listening. Cats of our ilk are often unfairly accused, although I've never understood why. I sometimes wonder if my so-called friends of the feline persuasion don't sometimes whisper lies into Mommy's ear to poison the air about me. But no, I refuse to think that one of our own kind is capable of such duplicity. More likely it's just Mommy's hormones all out of whack.

Oh, there's Mommy calling me. Not that I'll respond, naturally. But I guess I'll have to hide so she can come and "find" me. These people! Such simple pleasures.

Anyway, Merry Christmas to you and your crew. Has your mommy put up the tree for you guys yet? I'm getting mine this weekend. Honey and I are already looking forward to our traditional who-can-dismantle-the-tree-the-fastest contest. Boy, at the end of the day, there's nothing like a little good, clean competitive cat fun, is there?

Please promise me you'll be very wary of that wicked Weedwacker. I know it's no match for you, my fearless hero, but they're tricky and devious, those Weedwackers.

Yours forever,

Cleo

To: CleoTheDivine@att.net
From: TyroneTheGreat@aol.com
Subject: Of Soccer Trees and Tummy Rubs

My Dearest Cleo, *Ma chère, ma bonne amie,*

The Weedwacker! But of course! I apologize for not seeing it myself. You know, of course, that the word itself, *Weedwacker,* comes from the bent-nose phrase "to whack," i.e., to take out. To destroy. To shoot in the eye à la Moe Green. I should have suspected. . . .

That said, it was with great delight that I opened your holiday card, but alas, there was no food inside. I assume, of course, that a separate package is being forwarded as I write, filled to absolute brimming with mouse ears, salamander tails, bird wings, and other delicacies of the season. As for me, my gift giving this Christmas has been seriously curtailed by one very depressing factor: I am not allowed outside! In fact, none of us are, except of course Lucy the Dog, but we won't discuss that.

You see (and of course you do, as only you can fully under-stand and comprehend my plight) that, since I don't even have access to one as truculent and distasteful as a Stealth to do my bidding, i.e., shopping, *pour moi*, I have no way to obtain the happy, seasonal goodies I so desire to offer to you. Sad, *mais non?*

So here's the deal: I noticed, while hanging around the big white cold food box the other day that—in the colder part that makes all the smells go away—a big piece of, yes, you guessed it, turkey! I promise I will make every effort to dislodge it from the door shelf upon which it sits and—after allowing it to return to its normal temperature and scent—somehow get it to you. Should you choose to share it with your sister, that is your decision. Know it comes to you with love. And if there are a few bites missing here and there, I know you will understand.

As to the season: wow! Are these folk we live with crazy or what? First, my mommy brings into the house (can you imagine it?) a tree! No, not a plant nor a shrub nor a bunch of tasty flowers. A tree. In a pot with dirt and everything. Had you not mentioned in your previous missive the concept of the "Christmas Tree," I might have mistook her intent entirely. Now, I can't express to you how my heart was warmed at her kindness, but then she made it very clear: I am not to go near it. What? You bring into my home the perfect toy and ban me from the area? From the very room, in fact? I don't think so.

First, Mommy put these little stars on a string around the little tree and then a string of shiny glass beads that look like cranberries, but not as tasty (trust me, I have experience in this area. It involved a vet, a stomach pump, but I digress. . . .), and then a whole bunch of little round colored balls. *Wunderbar!* Let the soccer games begin! It was difficult, but with amazing feline paw dexterity, I removed several of the toys from the tree. LizzieBeth managed to create a distraction by deftly throwing up on the bedroom rug, which kept Mommy busy and away cleaning it up.

After performing that feat, LizzieBeth joined me at the tree. I knocked the shiny balls down to her, and she managed to get them away from the living room and into the family room, hiding them in her covered bed.

Anyway, after removing most of the toys—which I am nevertheless certain were meant for me—from the bottom of the tree, I took a nice long drink from the water dish under the tree, yanked down the string of beads (I wanted to make sure LizzieBeth would not have the misfortune of assuming, as I once did when I was oh, so very young, that they were edible and thus get very sick) and then tore a bit of the foil wrapped around the bottom of the tree, just for the fun of it. After all, it is the season to be jolly and nothing makes me more jolly than a few hours of unbridled destruction. Not to mention exhausted.

And as expected, Mommy went absolutely nuts! She shrieked like the proverbial banshee, then chased me around the house for what seemed like hours. Truth be told, it was so much fun, but I had to look scared or she doesn't enjoy it. Then she sat on the couch and just sighed. A short time later, after swallowing a few little round colored "candies" from a jar in the bathroom cabinet, she appeared to calm down. Then she went back into the living room and put the little stars and cranberries on a string back onto the little tree. She put more water into the dish (so thoughtful of her—I was just getting thirsty again) and then—lo and behold!—she found all new toys to put upon the lower branches of the little tree! I can't wait till it gets dark and Mommy goes to bed. . . .

So that, my little one, is the news from the hill. I do hope you and your sister and Stealth, as well as your mommy and daddy (and The Big Old Stupid Dog, I must grudgingly offer) have a wonderful holiday. I plan to spend the morning in the kitchen, tracking down and eating all the scraps that fall to the floor, and the afternoon on the living room couch, dozing to the meowing of the *Jingle Cats* CD (worthy of a Grammy, I assure you) and dreaming of soccer trees and tummy rubs.

With good wishes for the season,

Tyrone the Terrorist

To: TyroneTheGreat@aol.com
From: CleoTheDivine@att.net
Subject: Dick Clark, Tiaras, and Resolutions

Dearest Ami Tyrone,

It's New Year's Eve. The tiara I'm wearing highlights my striking eyes. And although I'm nibbling on shrimp pâté and sipping champagne as I watch Dick Clark on TV and wait for the big ball to drop down onto Times Square, I find myself feeling very sad, melancholy, and lonely. Perhaps it's simply a time for introspection, a time to take my emotional pulse.

The New Year is a signal for new beginnings. I've thought and thought about areas I need to improve, and I can think of none. Perhaps I must reach out, beyond myself, and concentrate on others less fortunate. Perhaps by my example, others will attain their dreams. But, Lordy, they have such a long row to hoe, so many imperfections to iron out. It's an enormous task to undertake, but I feel I am up to the challenge. And now that Mother Teresa is gone, well, someone must come in and fill the void. That someone might as well be *moi*. The Nobel Peace Prize would look stunning around my swanlike neck, don't you think? But if anyone thinks I'm going to wear that unstylish *schmatta*

It's New Year's Eve.
The tiara I'm wearing highlights
my striking eyes.

popularized by Mother Teresa, they are sadly mistaken. I will have to create my own saintly image.

So who is most in need of my largesse? Who needs the most help? That's easy. Mommy. She is deficient in so many areas; I could make her my lifetime project. Also, I'll commit to offering assistance to The Big Old Stupid Dog and that thug of a cat, Stealth. Just thinking about that trio is enough to send a body to bed, but I must be strong.

1. ENCOURAGE MOMMY TO IMPROVE HER LIFESTYLE. I know the more cynical reader—oh, not you, sweet Ty— might suggest that my motives for getting Mommy in shape are self-serving. There are even those who might think that the only reason I want Mommy around is because I need someone to open the cat food cans. Tears fill my eyes when I think that people might believe I am really that shallow. Damn! My mascara's running again. The truth is I can open the cans. I prefer not to, of course, because there's always the danger that I might cut myself and damage my beautiful, photogenic paw. And besides, why deprive Mommy of the task? It makes the poor dear feel needed.

And the garbage she throws into her body is simply shocking. Surely she realizes that foodstuffs with names like Yoo-Hoos, Ring Dings, and Ho Hos cannot have any real nutritional value.

A high protein diet is the key. I will pass along your excellent recipe for mouse ears. She needs to eat a more vitamin-rich diet, which could include such delicacies as lizard toes en brochette and fish-neck stew. I'll also allow her a small glass of caternet every evening and a snack of small anchovies (oops, that might be redundant).

But as the experts say, dieting alone isn't the answer. My mommy's going to have to get off her beloved couch and exercise. She always says jumping to conclusions is the only exercise she needs, but I'm afraid she's deluding herself. Does she really think this svelte body of mine comes without a hefty price tag? *Mais non*. What does she think I'm doing as I race through the house, leaping agilely and nimbly from bookcase to stereo to refrigerator top?

Brrr . . . A shudder just passed through my entire perfect body. You see, I got a mental image of my mommy leaping from bookcase to stereo to refrigerator. It was a truly heart-stopping image. Not a pretty picture at all. No, no, my mommy must find some other form of exercise.

2. HELP THE DOG FIND A HOBBY. You know, Tyrone, I am not a big fan of the canine species. They're so unruly and uncouth. But I must admit old Chester has, on occasion, tugged on my heartstrings. He's such an innocent. Granted, he's a little slow on the uptake, but there's still something about the critter that's rather endearing. Like a tattered, comfy old slipper you're loath to throw away. Maybe if he had something to occupy that pea brain of his. Master sleuthing is out of the question. So is petit point. Let me think, let me think. If given his druthers, loopy old Chester is perfectly content to just lie on the floor, staring vacantly at a blank wall. And drooling. His only other activity is sneezing as I stroll by. Do you have any idea how offensive doggy saliva is when it's sprayed all over your purrfect phurr? Well, maybe I can buy him one of those dog chew-toys—you know, the ones made out of pig's feet, lamb's lungs, and cow's hooves. Dogs seem to love chewing on them until they become all wet and slimy and gross. At least he'd be exercising his jaw. Well, it's something.

3. FIND A PROPER HOME FOR STEALTH. That cat's really getting on my nerves. He really is such a lowlife. It's not his fault, of course. We can't change genetics. (Well, as it

turns out, we can, but I don't think a philosophical discussion about cloning is in order right now.) What does Stealth know about Mozart and petits fours? No, he's more of a pickup-with-gun-rack kind of cat. I think I've found the perfect place for him. Montana. People in camouflage suits running around with guns, doing all that macho guy stuff. I think he'd be much happier there. Among his own kind. Out of the goodness of my heart and my own piggy bank, I purchased him a one-way ticket to a place called Bozeman. *Vaya con Dios, amigo.*

4. FIND A MEANINGFUL RELATIONSHIP. I know I said I was going to focus all my energy on others, but if I might be permitted one small self-indulgence, I would like a meaningful relationship. Someone who will drop me an e-mail just because. Someone with whom I can have an intelligent conversation. Someone who thinks the waltz is more elegant than the tush push. Hmmm . . . The more I think about it, Tyrone, someone just like you.

Oh, dear, have I been too bold?

With my heart all atwitter,

Cleo

To: CleoTheDivine@att.net
From: TyroneTheGreat@aol.com
Subject: Of Feral Felines and Niles Crane

My Dearest Cleo,

It is with great joy that I received your slight missive this afternoon. Imagining you sitting alone on New Year's Eve in your tiara practically broke my heart. There isn't any of that shrimp pâté left, is there? Well, just know I tried to get to you, but as luck would have it, there was an obstruction, a real reason I could not vacate my position in this house, not even for a moment. As you may or may not know, strange and terrible things have been going on here, and I fear all is out of control and careening toward the abyss.

For no discernible reason (for, I suggest, all reason has fled my own mommy's mind and spirit) this home, my sanctuary, the place in which I not only live but also reign supreme, has been invaded! Invaded, I tell you, by the cat from hell. Well, if not hell, purgatory, or maybe New Jersey. Whatever. This tiny waif of a critter, gray like ash, tiny of body and furtive of manner, was actually ENTICED by my own mommy into coming inside, whereupon she slammed the door behind him and announced he was now an indoor cat. Absolutely beside himself with terror, this nubbin of a feline then began to climb anything and everything in sight, hence the phrase, "climbing the walls." At least now I know where it comes from.

And do you know what Mommy has named him? Magic. Indeed!

Why my mommy decided it was time to induce this feral creature into my home I will never understand. Sure, she noticed the first day he showed up almost a year ago, pressing his tiny body up against our French doors, looking pathetic and frightened. But I saw it for the act it was right from the very start. One look at those sad little eyes and, before you could say "Fancy Feast," she was putting food out for him every day. Twice a day. Sometimes more. Okay, okay, so he was really skinny and could have used an extra meal or two. But then, when the rains came, she went out and bought him a little cottage and outfitted it with pillows and towels and a small lightbulb for heat. I swear, he was really comfortable out there. He could have lived out there FOREVER!

But no. I don't know if it was the coyotes who wander around up here, or the drop in temperature, or the fact that this "Magic" would disappear for days on end, driving Mommy to complete and utter distraction, but she moved the interloper inside.

After climbing the walls, Magic gave up and cowered in the bedroom corner. That lasted about three days. Then he began to venture forth, most notably into the kitchen. And he discovered the food dishes. Yes, it's true. He crept in, low to the ground, head shifting from right to left with furtive fury, and then slowly began to check out the wet-food dish, then the dry-food dish, my water dish and—get this—he went to MY litter box and USED IT! And what was Mommy's reaction to all this? She praised him.

Yeah, that's right. It was all "good Magic" and "what a good boy" kind of stuff. Nauseating.

To tell the truth, he is pathetic, but now this Niles Crane wannabe demands lap time. Yes, you heard me correctly, *ma cherie*, lap time. *My* lap time. Or what should be my lap time, were I so inclined to have lap time. At that time. Lap time.

And when I get into bed at night, you'll never guess—not in a million years. Well, yes, you're right—you did guess: Magic is already there. And, imagine this if you will—he hisses at me! At me! Being on the bed is my right, my privilege, my territory, my destiny manifested! He even reached out as if to scratch me! Well, I hissed right back and gave him the paw, I did. Oh, did that offend you? I'm sorry. Sometimes I forget myself. But I did, and I meant it.

Do you think I should just wander the house when Mommy is gone, opening those windows and doors I can reach and hope that Magic will make a dash for freedom? Or do you think, like so many formerly outdoor cats before him, he has come to realize he has fallen into the honey pot (MY HONEY POT!) and is here to stay? Oy, this is giving me a headache. I think I'd better go shred something just to calm down.

With all my heart (and the hope that a bit of the shrimp pâté remains),

Tyrone the Tremendous

To: TyroneTheGreat@aol.com
From: CleoTheDivine@att.net
Subject: Feline 101

𝒟ear 𝒯yrone, *Mon Cher,*

Goodness! You frightened me to death when you mentioned things were out of control and you felt you were careening toward the abyss. For a heart-stopping moment, I was sure you were going to do battle on my behalf with the Wicked Weedwacker. I don't deny it would have been a nice, romantic, heroic gesture on your part, but as it turns out you had other things on your mind—namely that Magic creature. What could your mommy have been thinking? Perchance, does she have any substance-abuse issues? I'm just wondering.

I was in exactly the same position with that dreadful Stealth creature. He lived outside, too. In fact, he lived in a tree right next to the garage. If I looked out the window in my office, I could see that darn cat up in the tree grinning down at me. As a writer, I'm always looking for unusual characters to populate my literary landscapes, but then I feared a crazed cat grinning out of a tree was just not a credible, sympathetic character.

So imagine my surprise when Mommy informed Honey and me

just the other day that Stealth was going to become an indoor cat. Like you, I don't know what prompted that move.

From what I can discern, there are only two approaches to this pesky problem. The first, and for *moi* the most direct, technique is what I refer to as the rip-the-welcome-mat-from-under-their-paws approach. Yes, it's harsh. Yes, it's tough love. Yes, it's effective. Basically, you must make the interloper feel unwelcome, unwanted, and unloved. Tell him at every opportunity what a poor excuse for a feline he is: untalented, stupid, and ugly. Keep reinforcing the notion of how unworthy and unhappy he is. Keep reminding him of the pleasures of the great outdoors, of all the catly activities he will be giving up. Withholding food and water is another technique that often works. Let's say the interloper has found a place within the house to call his own. (I am assuming of course that you would have removed all pillows, blankets, etc., and claimed them for yourself.) So let's say that all that remains for the interloper is a potted plant. He squeezes his pathetic little body around the petunia. When he gets up, you put nails in the soil. See how comfortable he is then!

You must understand, of course, that I have never resorted to such severe actions, but I have heard of interlopers fleeing from the house, wanting more than anything to be outdoor cats again. And think what a favor you would be doing if you helped this Magic thing regain his freedom. I've always believed Stealth was much happier in that lousy tree. Now that he's in the house, I don't see him grinning anymore.

I should warn you, however, that your mommy might misinterpret your actions and blame you for running the cat out of town on a rail. Mommies always take the side of the undercat, and I guarantee you she'll accuse you of being a bully and a lousy host to boot. Who needs that?

So perhaps a better approach might be—just to keep your mommy's hormones in check—what I call the buddy system. In a show of magnanimous generosity, you offer to help the cat from the moment he crosses the threshold. You teach him the rules of the house. In other words, YOUR rules. Of course he's welcome to eat exactly the same food you eat. AFTER YOU HAVE FINISHED, OF COURSE. He can claim a comfy spot AS LONG AS IT ISN'T YOUR FAVORITE HIDEY HOLE. And you must caution him to keep his grubby little paws off your catnip toys. Gently explain that catnip is a controlled, addictive substance, and you certainly don't want him traveling down the "dark and twisty road" you've been traveling.

Besides getting the interloper to conform to your rules, your mommy will love you for your generous spirit and might give you some extra lap time or a special treat.

I know it's a pain in the derrière, but until you can either push him through the door or convince your mommy that he is single-pawedly destroying the house and putting the other critters in danger, I fear this is how you must proceed.

Feeling your pain,

Cleo

To: CleoTheDivine@att.net
From: TyroneTheGreat@aol.com
Subject: Pyramus and Thisbe

My Dearest, Most Empathetic Cleo,

What wonderful suggestions! Make him conform or throw the bum out! On his bum. As it were. I must think about this. But, again, I fear, my attention has been torn from my priority by yet another catastrophe: my mommy has been looking for a new place to live—a smaller place! What then, I ask you? All of us crammed into some tiny little cardboard hovel, with dirt on the floor, a hot plate, and a Denver Broncos Styrofoam cooler for liquids and mayonnaise—we'll all die for sure—and a bathroom outdoors? I grow faint at the very image of it. We are doomed, doomed, I tell you!

I suspect it's time for all of us to shout, "I'm mad as hell and I won't take it anymore!" Though, from us, it comes out something like: "Meow Merrorrow mi mellllll, meh Meow orrorrorooowh meeerrwhhhhow." (Do you find the longer you're here on this planet, the more our native Felinese slips from our memory? First the vocabulary goes, then the syntax, then the declensions. . . .)

42

Please know, dear Cleo, that I applaud your oh-so-generous New Year's resolutions for all those sad souls in your life. As for your mommy, don't let her lose weight. Not an ounce! Just don't do it. There will be less of her and if there is less of her, you might find yourself the one left out of the kneading sessions, losing out to that demanding Honey.

But, as for Stealth, admit it, my love, is this not a case of a woman scorned? Admittedly, I am more handsome, more virile (or, I would be if it weren't for that pesky little Lorena Bobbitt thing my vet did, the ghoul) and more fun than Stealth, so there really is no competition. Not that I want any. Nor fear any. And not that it matters one way or the other. Unless, of course . . .

Okay, okay, I confess: you are the one who has wrapped her paws around my fat, fuzzy heart. Yes, as with Romeo and Juliet (or was it Pyramus and Thisbe?), our families are keeping us apart. Though, if none of your suggestions work to restrain, re-train, or return to the wild that Uriah Heep-ish Magic, I swear, I'll find a way to get to you, my love. And I'll move in. For good.

Avec tout mon coeur,
Tyrone the Triumphant

To: TyroneTheGreat@aol.com
From: CleoTheDivine@att.net
Subject: Romeo and Juliet Redux

My Dearest Tyrone,

When I read your latest missive, I must admit my knees buck-led and I swooned. (By the way, when I glance down at my shapely legs, I don't seem to have knees. Do you have knees? How come bees have knees and I don't?) My mommy picked up my beautiful but limp body and put me to bed. She pleaded with me to eat. Finally, just to appease her, I told her perhaps I could gag down a dish of mouse ears, but Mommy draws the line at rodent parts. I point out, however, she has no trouble blithely tossing chicken parts around. Like chicken parts are *so* attractive!

No doubt you are curious about the cause of my buckling knees and swooning. You said you were MOVING, Tyrone!!! Where?! The nether regions of the universe? Pacoima? Akron? My constitution is far too frail for you to drop these bombshells on me. You must write me immediately to assure me that you are still in my neighborhood, in my universe, in my zip code. I would be devastated if that were not the case.

I must admit I was absolutely shocked you perceived me as a

cat who had been scorned. I am NOT scorned. Ever. And certainly not by a gangster like Stealth. Oh sure, I admit I'm a sucker for the strong, silent type. But the only reason he's silent is because he has absolutely nothing worthwhile to say. Not a single bon mot will ever escape his lips. When you really study him, you realize he's not even particularly attractive. He's shaped rather like a *Bûche de Nöel*. And I don't much like his friends. He hangs out with a rough crowd. Too many fedoras and black-on-black shirts and ties for my taste. And his nose looks like it's been broken one too many times. Also, I'm not real comfortable with cats whose business cards read "Enforcer."

Non, non, mon ami. If anyone has ever captured my heart, it is you. I look at you and it's as if I'm looking at myself. I can pay you no greater compliment.

Please send me your new address immediately, and let me know how you're progressing with Magic the Wimp.

With all my heart,

Cleo

To: CleoTheDivine@att.net
FROM: TyroneTheGreat@aol.com
SUBJECT: Educating Magic

𝒟earest 𝒞leo, the Light of My Life, the Sun of My Sky, the Chocolate Chip of My Cookie,

I know I should have written sooner, but quite a bit has been going on, and you know how hard it is to find time to put paw to keyboard. That said, there is much mews.

First, fear not, little one, for I am quite certain that my mommy is not moving us very far. She is much too fond of her own food stores, her own dry cleaners, her own restaurants, and on and on and on (are these people persons functionally fixed or what?) to even consider an entirely new neighborhood. No, I suspect we will simply be closer to the foot of the hill rather than at the top of it, all the better to be near the action, my dear.

Now, I have taken your suggestions re Magic, that is, train the critter or throw him out, to heart—out of consideration for Mommy's feelings and because I couldn't manage, with my big, manly paws, to unlock any of the doors or windows—and decided to train him.

His education began right away. First, I had to explain how, come first light or even a bit before, LizzieBeth and I jump up on Mommy's bed and tap her on the nose until she wakes up and gets us our food. However, I had to explain that, as an example of her gross inconsideration, she goes into the porcelain and tile room and sits down for a bit, brushes her teeth, and sometimes—gall of gall—takes a shower first. But then she finally drags her sleep-deprived bod (like it's my fault she can't sleep through our performances of Cirque du Feline on the bed at night) into the kitchen, opens the mystical cans that say such things as "chicken," "duck," "salmon," etc., but don't really have any of those critters in them, and we chow down. I also had to explain that, if patient, Mommy also sets out fresh dry food, a nice big bowl of it, and a dish of fresh filtered water. As we are eating, she then cleans out our litter box, so when we are done we have a fresh and clean box to mess up. I especially like being first in as there is lots and lots of nice, fresh and dry litter and I can kick it around with my hind legs and paws and throw a great deal of it around, if I am lucky and my aim is true, out and onto the carpet.

Then, full and happy, I led Magic out to the living room and directed him to take up a position on one of the couches. I explained that we must sleep for most of the day. (Can you imagine having to explain this to a fellow feline? I swear it's all true.) We then eat again at four or so, and nap until just around the time Mommy is really tired and heads for bed. Then we arise with a snap and begin to dash around the house in no discernible pattern and for no particular reason. (I know, I know: we know the reasons, but we cannot reveal all of our secrets to the nonfelines, can we?) I then had to give Magic a tour, showing him that there are dozens of closets and piles of clothes, drawers filled with great stuff, file cabinets, bookcases, kitchen cupboards filled with metal pots and pans, tissue boxes, and rolls and rolls of toilet paper and paper towels and, of course, our toy box! It's full of stuffed animals, balls, string, birds and mice, and lots and lots of catnip-filled toys, as I'm sure you recall, Cleo my love. It's absolute heaven, though Magic seemed confused. Do you suppose he's never had any toys of his own? If that be true, then I fear I have found a reason to feel sorry for him. Mommy says he was a wild cat, born outside and never had a mommy of his own. No mommy, no toys, I think she was trying to say. Ah, the tragedy and perils of living in the wild. Even if it is the wilds of the Hollywood Hills.

Now, after all this, do you think Magic was grateful? Do you think he showed his gratitude in some tasty food-related way? No. In fact, quite the opposite. He challenged me! Yes, you heard correctly. He decided he should be Alpha Cat. And what did I do, you ask? Did I take it? Did I accept a demotion in my very own home? In front of Lucy the Dog and LizzieBeth, no less? What do you think? Of course not. So we had a brawl. Yes, we did. We arranged to meet right after dinner in the TV room. We faced each other, each of us up on our hind legs. We threatened each other with limp and swishing paws, and then the action began. He leapt for my throat, and I sidestepped neatly, letting him careen into the coffee table. He recovered quickly and came at me again, but stopped to posture for a bit. And then more brawling. And while I did manage to scratch his nose pretty good, he got me, too. But before there was too much blood or fur, Mommy came running in (I guess we were a bit on the loud side, what with our shrieking and all) and screamed at us. Good heavens, that woman can raise the roof when she wants to. She tossed Magic into the office and me into the bedroom. And then she tended to each of us in turn, putting this awful-tasting antibacterial goo on our cuts and scratches, a bandage on my cheek, and one on Magic's ear. We looked ridiculous. But I think we've managed to settle our differences. I'm top cat, and now he accepts it. I hope. Sigh. Just another day in paradise.

Dearest Cleo, know you are always in my thoughts, just above salmon and turkey bits,

Tyrone the InTrepid

TO: TyroneTheGreat@aol.com
FROM: CleoTheDivine@att.net
SUBJECT: A Cat's Life

Dear Tyrone, My Chunka, Chunka Burning Love,

My poor Tyrone! Your handsome profile marred by a scratch and a bandage! I hope your mommy gave you a treat for your heroism. Or did she blame you for starting the fight?

You sound like a wonderful teacher, Tyrone. A kind of butch Anne Sullivan. It is obvious Magic has not been brought up well, and I am quite certain a finishing school is not listed on his résumé.

I love the structure of your day. It's practically poetic. Like you, I have designed my day so it's efficient, has its own rhythms and music, and of course, allows for plenty of beauty sleep.

Being nocturnal animals as we are, I make the supreme sacrifice of staying awake until I can rouse my mommy and daddy. Yes, I know about those alarm clocks, but you can't trust them; you could have a power blackout and your mommy and daddy could sleep till the cows come home. (By the way, Tyrone, have you EVER seen the cows come home? No, me neither. Nor have I heard the fat lady sing.) I try to wake them up around 5:30 A.M.

50

There are many ways of waking up parents, but I have found the most direct, while perhaps not the most creative, methods are still the most effective: using my mommy's chest as a trampoline, I jump up and down, higher and higher I go until she wakes up; or I gently caress her face and if she doesn't awaken, I slap her really hard; or sometimes I like to go to a high surface and hurl things down to the floor. If the item hurled crashes, both my mommy and daddy sit up so fast you'd think they'd been shot out of a cannon. That's actually pretty funny to see. Nothing I like better than starting out the day with a good laugh.

After breakfast, it's time to exercise. First, I like to stretch. Really stretch. My slinky, svelte body is like taffy, and I can stretch it into these incredibly long, skinny lengths and impossible positions. Mommy says I look like a pipe cleaner with attitude. After that linear stretch, I arch my back to work out any spinal kinks. In this particular pose, I look like a very attractive tunnel.

Now it's time for the cardiovascular portion of my regimen. There's some leeway here. I actually prefer track and field events, in particular hurdles and the broad jump. I race like the wind, jumping over the Big Old Stupid Dog, coffee tables, Mommy horizontal on the couch. (She says she's solving the problems of the world, but it looks a lot like sleeping to me, what with the snoring, drooling, and all.) That is followed by the broad jump, where I sail through the air from bookcase to stereo cabinet to refrigerator top. I like to imagine how my beautiful body looks as it soars. It must be a thrilling sight.

Afterward, it's time for cooldown and refreshments. I groom my fur and have a little bottled water. Next, it's time for contemplation and reflection. Sometimes I contemplate black holes and infinity; other times I consider the ailing Asian markets; and on

*My svelte, slinky body
is like taffy, and I can stretch it
into these incredibly long,
skinny lengths. . . .*

more than one occasion I have pondered the many ways to eliminate/terminate The Big Old Stupid Dog.

I am brought out of my reverie by the sound of a can being opened. I'd know that sound anywhere. It's albacore tuna, water packed, and Mommy's making herself a sandwich. Is she thinking about us? But of course not. However, I've found if I nag really long and hard and maybe step directly into the can, she'll part with a little flaked tuna au jus. The trick here is to make sure you have all the tuna for yourself and don't have to share it with your siblings. I've found if I create a little dissension between Honey and Stealth, I pretty much have the tuna to myself as they vie for position of top cat. (Fine, you guys be top cat; I'll take the tuna.)

During the afternoon, I allow a little time for myself. First I watch my favorite soap opera, "One Furball to Give." What that hunk Rick Rack sees in that little harlot, Velveteen, is beyond me. Sure she looks okay now, but she'll turn to fat in no time. You just wait and see. The rest of the afternoon is spent on grooming (manicure, pedicure, etc.), the everyday things a girl must do to look gorgeous. (Tuesdays I devote an entire day to grooming. That's when I do the whisker dying, deep fur-conditioning, and body wraps. I've found the seaweed wrap is particularly effective. Tasty, too.) Then I answer my fan mail and autograph photos.

After I finish my dinner, I like to jump up on the table and onto Mommy's and Daddy's plates and check out what they're having. Naturally, they scream at me, but I can tell their hearts really aren't in it. The truth is they find me adorable—as who would not?

The evenings are spent with the family. There are so many activities to participate in, I barely know which to select. Shall I make it more challenging for Daddy to complete his crossword puzzle by sitting in the middle of it and trying to wrest the pencil out of his hand? No, tonight I think I'll help Mommy wrap that birthday gift. First, I jump into the gift box, tossing those Styrofoam peanuts all over the living room. After Mommy extricates me from the box and retrieves the peanuts, I unroll the wrapping paper and bedeck everything in sight—including The Big Old Stupid Dog—with the gaily colored ribbon. Mommy threatens to wrap me in a box and give me away. But instead, she puts a stick-on bow on my head and tells me how cute I am.

All too soon it's Mommy's and Daddy's bedtime. I take my rightful place right between them—at the head of the bed. The Big Old Stupid Dog, while taking up more space, has the less desirable position at the foot of the bed. When they're sound asleep, I carefully, quietly get out of bed. This is when I devote myself to my creative-writing pursuits. I really must think about starting my autobiography soon; I can't keep putting off those publishers. And this is the time, dearest Tyrone, when I write to you. And think about when we can be together again. My, how I do long for you, you big spotted hunk.

Yours forever,

Cleo

To: CleoTheDivine@att.net
From: TyroneTheGreat@aol.com
Subject: Jane Austen, Wes Craven, and Torquemada

Dearest Cleo,

Ah, your day sounds as crowded and stressful as mine. I keep thinking, when things get far too doggy for me to handle, that I just might try to get my paws on those little blue pills my mommy runs to whenever we drive her to the brink. I don't know what they are, as my doctorese isn't that good, but they sure do put a smile on Mommy's face—albeit not for at least forty-five minutes. Perhaps next time. Actually, when I think about it, now would be a good time. Why, you ask? Let me explain.

I've worked for years, dammit, to become the absolute center of attention and then what happens? Apparently Mommy first noticed, about a week or so ago, that there was a glop of vomit on the floor, mauve vomit tinged with blood. I tried to inform my mommy that Magic was the source, but wouldn't you know, she just couldn't figure out which one of us was upchucking, so she ran around like a crazy person checking each of our mouths, seeing if we had blood in it, I guess, or a dead bird or rat—I'm not sure. Anyway, we were all clean, so no charges could be filed. Oops, wrong report. I mean, no blood, no victim.

Then, over the next few days, more of that glop was found deposited around various parts of the house. Now, were it left to *moi*, I would have realized that none of this type of disgusting behavior—not to mention vomit—had been left about before Magic arrived, so via a rather unsophisticated process of elimination, it must be him. Solution: dump the ungrateful pet wannabe in some game preserve, pet shelter, or coyote den. But did that happen? No. Was I even asked for my opinion? No, of course not.

After a few days of Magic's leaving said hints at least as subtle as bread crumbs from the witch's cottage, he came to the reluctant conclusion he had to take matters into his own hands, or paws, as appropriate. So, last Friday after breakfast, Magic waited until Mommy was comfortably seated at the kitchen table sipping her first cup of morning coffee. Magic knew now was the moment: he just had to let her know he was the proud source of the bloody vomit. So he meowed in his most pathetic manner (or so he thought), and when she glanced down at him, he threw back his little head and vomited. Lots and lots. Red and pink. And mauve. So there you have it, Mommy. Now can you deduce from whom this ooze originates? Yes, he threw up right in front of her!

Now, Cleo, *mon petit chou*, we both know very well that any vomiting must be done in secret, so as to drive our people absolutely mad in their attempt to discover the source. But Magic broke the rules, he did, and I am here to gleefully report he paid for it. After a fashion.

Well, you never would have expected Mommy's reaction! It was absolutely Jane Austen and Wes Craven, all rolled into one.

In the blink of an eye, she reached down, scooped Magic up and with Magic still under her arm, tore into our bedroom and threw on some clothes. Enough, I thought. When do I get some attention? No sooner said than done. She bent down and scooped me up, this time right alongside Magic who was, by now, wrapped in a blanket. She tore out of the house and into the truck. And all this before 8:00 A.M.!

I don't know for sure if Mommy took me along for the company or because she's terrified of leaving me alone in the house, but off I went with her and Magic. She was in such a hurry she didn't even grab those ominous things they call "crates," and so we were both "free to move about the cabin," as it were. I, of course, took up residence on the front seat, and bracing my front paws against the dashboard, I hung on for dear life. We were moving with great speed, but the view was marvelous! The window was open a little bit, and the wind was shooshing around, my fur standing straight up and my ears flopping in the wind. *Wheee-eeee!*

Then, without warning, the journey came to an end. We, Magic and I, were taken into this place, this room, which carried the light scent of disinfectant and urine. Dog urine. Uh-ooo. Yes, you guessed right. It was the vet's. We waited eternally in that room for what was certainly at least half an eternity. Finally we were ushered into this even smaller room, and Magic was set upon a table, where Dr. Ciganek, my vet, wearing a most unfashionable white jacket (and this, so long after Labor Day), began to examine him.

Oh, humiliation of humiliations! Dr. Ciganek put a thermometer into Magic's ass! Now, I'm sure you can understand when I say I never allow that sort of thing myself. I just wiggle and waggle and set my butt firmly down onto that cold examining table,

I, of course, took up residence on the front seat, and bracing my front paws against the dashboard, I hung on for dear life.

hissing and spitting, and eventually Dr. "C" gives up. But Magic was totally unprepared. And in the thermometer went! I must have laughed myself silly. I almost collapsed and threw up from the sheer sight of Magic's horrified and embarrassed face. Can you picture it? And, that done, the vet then pried open Magic's mouth and gazed inside. And then he began to poke and prod that wimpy little gray mass endlessly. It was too good.

Then came the horror to end all horrors: the doc stuck a needle into Magic's paw and drew blood! Even I had to look away. As if Magic hadn't lost enough with all his vomiting, but this Torquemada clone had to get some more. You never know who the vampires are, I always say. Anyway, that done, he ushered us out. Back home, I got to parade around and let LizzieBeth know how special I was as I'd been the only one treated to the ride with the ill one, but LizzieBeth was wary. And, as usual, her instincts were right on. While I figured Magic's disgusting vomiting shtick would cause Mommy to throw the bum right out on his tiny rump, LizzieBeth was convinced this would only endear him to Mommy more. How do you females do it?

Okay, so later that same day, I heard Mommy on the phone telling your very own mommy of our adventure. And do you know what she said? She told your mommy that Magic is stressed. Stressed?! Can you imagine? He lives in an eight-room house filled with pillows and curtains and couches and beds and food and litter boxes and tons and tons of toys and he's stressed? Oh, puhleeze . . . And stressed over what? Is he the one who had his territory impinged upon? I think not. If anyone has the right to be stressed, it's me.

So, bottom line, that little pile of pink-puking gray fur and fibers is now served more food more often. He has to take his medicine, I admit, but then my very own mommy holds and comforts him, as if he needs it. I'm the one who's stressed. I swear, I'm about ready to swallow glass so I, too, will start to vomit blood.

Well, I am getting drowsy, as I've been up for the better part of an hour now.

So, as I settle in for another nap and drift off, pondering what to do about Magic the Intruder, I wonder . . . I wonder . . .

Cleo dearest, do you have any tiny tools? Some lumber, some wire, a bare handful of nails? And lots and lots of postage . . . ?

If so, my passion, my tiny chicken breast of my heart, my salmon dumpling, send immediately. As for now, I must leave you, if only on paper, for you will always remain in my heart. And with that happy thought, I shall bid you adieu.

Avec tout mon coeur,
Tyrone the Tyrannosaurus

To: TyroneTheGreat@aol.com
From: CleoTheDivine@att.net
Subject: And the Gold Goes To . . .

My Dearest Tyrone,

You poor dear. You sound absolutely undone. Magic seems to have not only turned your world upside down, but it appears he's able to snap his little toes and your mommy comes running to do his bidding. The next time you're sitting on your mommy's head, you might want to check under her bangs and see if "sucker" is printed on her forehead.

And the temerity to vomit right in front of your mommy! It was obviously a blatant attempt to attract attention that shows neither creativity nor cleverness. Perhaps classes in subtlety and finesse are in order.

Magic is sorely mistaken if he thinks for one little second that he's in your league in the attention-getting department. Let's face it, *mon ami*, if attention-getting were an Olympic event, surely you and I would be gold medalists. Here are a few of the techniques I've been perfecting over the years.

My particular favorite is escaping. While my mommy is out of the room, I harass the dog so badly that he begs to go outside.

When my mommy lets him out, I streak out right behind him. Of course Mommy starts screaming at me. Now, here's what I do. I lie down on the grass real flat. I don't move a muscle. She comes slowly toward me. At this point, she's feeling pretty confident that I'm within easy grasp. As she reaches down to pick me up, I scurry away. If I'm lucky, she falls right on her nose. I leap onto the high fence and watch her as she picks herself up, plucking Bermuda grass out of her hair. How I do laugh! I can continue this little game for hours, running from one end of the fence to the other. As she approaches me, I sit very still, and then as she reaches for me, I scurry off in the opposite direction. I do this until I become bored. And think of all the lap time I've deprived the other felines of. I rub my delicate little paws together in glee. Then I let her "capture" me. It makes her feel like she's won.

Also effective, as you've mentioned before, is the disappearing act we pull as our mommies try to herd us into the cat carriers for a trip to the vet (ugh!). I like to fit myself into someplace really small and dark. I just sit there and she yells my name over and over again, her voice becoming increasingly desperate. Sometimes she tries to lure me out with a can of white albacore tuna. It takes discipline to resist that tempting treat, but it's worth the effort. Then to add a *Gaslight*ing element to the exercise, just when she reaches the breaking point—when her voice becomes really high-pitched and annoying, a thin patina of perspiration covering her forehead and she threatens that I'm going to be the major ingredient in the cassoulet she's preparing—I appear in the middle of the living room, sitting very still, nonchalantly licking my paws, as if I'd been there for hours. I give her one of those what-is-your-problem, are-you-having-one-of-those-menopause-moments looks. Very effective.

There are less fatiguing ways to get your mommy's attention.

Although many of these techniques are considered clichéd, they are still very effective. When Mommy is lying on the sofa reading a book, I place myself between the book and her face. Or sometimes I sit on the darn book. Just depends on how I feel.

Then there's the fur thing. I think it's perfect that I have a lot of white fur and a lot of multicolored fur. First, and most important, it's very becoming, and second, with this particular color combo, I can shed my white fur on Mommy's dark clothes and my multicolored fur on her light clothes. She never leaves the house without a large part of me going with her. I am always close to her heart—and every other part of her anatomy, for that matter.

And of course who among us hasn't resorted to the tried and true crying piteously for no reason whatsoever? It will bring my mommy running every single time. That one's almost too easy.

What other techniques have you found to be particularly effective?

Although I don't have a new interloper to contend with, I am facing my own angst at the moment. Did I mention to you I've been writing haiku of late? The reason I chose this particular form of self-expression is because nobody else seems to be doing it. My mommy's plumber, gardener, and the roof guy are all writing screenplays, but I never hear anyone say they're writing haiku.

Now, if I had my way, I'd pattern my life after Emily Dickinson. I'd wear a long black dress with a virginal white Peter Pan collar, and I'd sit around waiting to be visited by the muse. When the muse showed up—my muse looks very much like you, my dearest Tyrone—I'd pick up my quill (after snacking on the bird from which it came, of course) and write my poetry. How idyllic!

But alas, Mommy has bought a new computer. Writing haiku on a computer just doesn't seem right. Like painting the Sistine

For Tyrone on Valentine's Day

You're the cat's meow
The scratching post of my soul
Catnip of my heart
avec tout mon amour,
Cleo

Chapel with an air compressor. And this computer has real attitude. When I write to you, a dancing paper clip gambols across my screen, asking me if I need help in writing this letter. That's right. A dancing paper clip. As if I needed help from a paper clip! What next? Is a trapeze-flying stapler going to appear to ask if I need help composing my haiku?

I feel it is the duty of the artist to always "push the envelope," but this is one of those phrases I don't understand. What exactly is the big deal about pushing the envelope? I push envelopes, papers, books, and magazines to the floor all the time just to get my mommy's attention. As an artist I don't like to always do everything according to the book. (What book? I never got that book.) Sometimes I don't feel like writing in complete sentences. or using a capital letter at the beginning of the sentence. or using any punctuation at all You know what happens? That paper clip appears on my screen to chastise me! Just who does he think he is? And does he not realize to whom he is speaking? Good God, does that creature not know his station?

Now, what to do about Magic? I think the simplest, most straightforward solution is still your best bet. Granted it's a variation of the escape technique, but if it works . . . ? Just before your mommy is expecting company, why don't you throw up in the living room? That will make your mommy crazy. She'll scurry around to clean up the mess. While she's so occupied, I'd get Lucy the Dog to open the back door, then I'd just shove Magic out. He'll be a coyote snack in no time at all.

Oh, Tyrone, I wish we were sitting together holding paws. How can we make that happen?

A bientôt, mon cher,

Cleo

My Dearest Cleo,

Ah, time passes far too quickly . . . whether or not you're having any fun.

And before I forget, I want to thank you so much for the Valentine's Day card. Did you get my gift of boxed salmon? No? Hmmm . . . Someone must have eaten it.

First, and I must reluctantly get this out of the way, Magic's tests came back and he is medically all right. About this I have admittedly mixed feelings. On the one hand, were he sick, he might die. But then Mommy would spend a great deal of time tending him, time taken away from me. And, I must reluctantly admit, I'm getting accustomed to his rather timid ways. So I suppose I am pleased he is healthy, though he may well continue to vomit due to "stress." Yeah. Right. At least he hasn't encroached upon my relationship with you, dear Cleo. Nor will I ever let him! (That was me letting out a mighty, threatening roar. I wish you could have heard it. It was truly impressive.)

Further, I must admit I was absolutely charmed by your instructions regarding attention-getting devices. Yet I must point out that you tend to focus on the hide-in-plain-sight methods. While always guaranteed to annoy and, therefore, focus attention on oneself, I myself prefer the hide-out-of-sight shenanigans.

For example, this past Sunday, my mommy, who is still trying to remove us from this house and move us into a place she insists will be cozier (read: smaller), was holding another Open House as part of her attempt to sell the only home I have ever known. And what role do I and my siblings play in all this? None. Now, I am perfectly capable of pointing out the highlights: the office bathroom tub where LizzieBeth prefers to pee; the place under the bed—just out of Mommy's reach—where one can store old dry food, fur balls, and dirty underwear; the woodwork where Magic often urinates; the spot on the rug where, after I delicately relieved myself of a particularly large and spectacular fur ball (my trajectory was truly impressive), an especially nasty stain remained. And then, in a valiant attempt to remove the stain, Mommy removed the color. From the carpet. Forever. I prefer to think of that spot as a tie-dyed ode to the sixties. But no. Mommy had different plans.

I should have begun to suspect something was afoot when she first gathered up four small blankets, all fresh from the dryer, disappeared into the living room, and then farther into the guest bedroom, reappearing a short time later at the back of the house amidst a sea of—dare I say it?—plastic.

Yes, you guessed it: she had removed all four of our carriers and set them in the front entryway. We all knew we had to run, and run we did. But, as one might expect, Magic and I were faster than little LizzieBeth, and she was scooped up. And then she disappeared. The dog was next. I grew afraid. Very, very afraid. What to do . . . What to do . . .

So, with LizzieBeth and Lucy the Dog MIA, I took action. First, I did a quick survey of the remaining and available rooms. Knowing that Magic was under the clothes in the laundry basket in the walk-in closet, I knew only the office bathroom, the family room, and kitchen were left available to me. This was not good. I knew Mommy would probably recall but a few weeks back when— again pulling a disappearing act—I managed to open the office bathroom vanity door, climb in quickly so the door would swing shut behind me (all the better to make anyone assume no one was in there), clamber over the mountain of toilet paper, up and into the inside top drawer. Yes, it was quite small, especially for someone of my muscular build, but I managed to hunker down and stay quiet. But I was discovered when, much to my chagrin, Mommy tried to open the drawer. I was too big. I overflowed. The drawer would not open. And I was found out. So scratch the office bathroom.

The kitchen? No. Mommy had long ago scoped out my hiding places there. That left the family room.

I studied the family room. I knew Magic would occupy Mommy a bit longer, but time was growing short. And I needed a hiding place. One large enough so I wouldn't get cramped, yet not so large that its location would leap into Mommy's mind. It had to be warm and relatively flat. And, while I didn't want it so enclosed that I could not escape (I still shudder recalling the infamous suitcase incident), I needed to make sure it would hide me from sight.

Again, from the bedroom, I heard Mommy entreating Magic to come out. From my future hiding place, I spied her retreating into the kitchen, then moving back to the bedroom—this time carrying the bright blue broom that often terrorizes LizzieBeth and Magic. (Though not me. I'm not afraid of sissy things like that.

But I was discovered when, much to my chagrin, Mommy tried to open the drawer.

Not me. Not ever . . . Well, maybe once. Or twice. But who's counting?) Anyway, she closed the door, enclosing her and Magic within the confines of her bedroom. I heard hissing. I heard shouting. And then I heard the door to her bathroom close.

Once more, her footsteps approached. I quickly disappeared

into my spot. Ah, perfect. I could see from a small space to the side, yet I was snug, comfortable, and—best of all—out of sight. Mommy opened the bedroom door, walked out the double doors, and disappeared. A beat, and she returned, carrying the pink carrier. The one with the firm lock. She meant business.

Again she disappeared into the bedroom, and farther into the bathroom. Imagine, if you will: one mommy in a shabby, formerly lavender robe, the bottom button missing and the butt area practically worn out, trapped in one small bathroom with Magic the Terrified. She had only a broom and an open carrier to accomplish her task. Did she arise victorious? Well, to hear Magic tell it, she was a crazy woman with the broom, and he outfoxed (pardon the use of that semicanine reference, but it seems appropriate) Mommy by slipping past her and hiding out in the carrier. God, he's dumb. Anyway, a few moments later, Mommy emerged from the bathroom and bedroom hoisting the now-loaded pink carrier. I could see Magic's face pressed up against the wire mesh door, his paws clutching the bars. It was pathetic. He was too beaten down to even meow. (Though to hear him tell it, he didn't meow because he didn't want to give Mommy the satisfaction, and he was just clutching the bars because Mommy was giving him a bumpy ride. Whatever.)

Mommy returned. The double doors to the living room were now open, and I could hear the incessant meowing and shrying of my siblings, now trapped and caged like, well, animals. It gives me big tail just to think about it. She then called my name. I became smaller. She called. And called. And called. She then disappeared into the bedroom, reemerged dressed (in a most fetching outfit, one that I, with my wonderfully fluffy white fur, love to sit upon: a black slacks and top ensemble) and a bit annoyed, if you'll indulge me in some amateur analysis. Again, she called me. What am I, a fool? No, this was my hiding place, and this is where I will stay, I affirmed.

I would not reveal my location upon pain of, well, I don't really want to suffer any real pain, but I would consider giving up my little white mouse, the one I bit the tail and ears off last year. But that's as far as I might go.

Mommy then began a search of the room, and what I could not see I could hear: cabinets and drawers opening and closing, climbing and crawling about on the floor, seeking this very feline under chairs and beds and couches. It was very amusing. Then, after almost half an hour, she did something very strange. She left. Not completely, of course, but she did leave. She went out the front door (I'd know that sound anywhere), and then began to load my siblings, in their carriers, into the back of our rather tacky red truck. She was gone for a few minutes, and then she returned to the family room. Somehow, I sense she suspected I was there, but she could not find me. She called me again, then warned that she had to leave. Time was up. And I would be left alone to deal with the human interlopers. The moment of truth: what would I do?

Now, dearest Cleo, you might well be wondering: where was that handsome rascal hiding? Well, beg and plead, my dearest, and I'll tell you. . . .

With much anticipation regarding your response,

Tyrone the Terminator

Diskette II

To: TyroneTheGreat@aol.com

From: CleoTheDivine@att.net

Subject: *Die Hard, Cliffhanger,* and Tenterhooks

My Dear Little Houdini,

Oh stop! You must not tease me in this cruel fashion! You have me on absolute tenterhooks! (What exactly is a tenterhook, by the way?) Just how, you little devil, did you manage to evade your mommy?

Knowing you, you devised some wickedly diabolical plan to escape being scooped up and hurled into the dreaded blue carrier. In the tradition of Bruce Willis and Sly Stallone, you probably fashioned a tenterhook out of a paper clip and some string, hoisted it over the chandelier, used it to rappel yourself over to the air-conditioning duct. Using a tiny little screwdriver from your well-equipped tool belt, you unscrewed the grate, jumped in, scampered through the ducts until danger had passed. No doubt, you even had the time and resources to catch a couple of mice and probably even a few z's.

Alas, I don't have those manly skills. I remember on one unfortunate occasion where I felt it was necessary to hide from my very own mommy. I don't remember the exact details, but I seem to recall it had something to do with a little Lalique cat, which somehow got hurled to the floor from the coffee table and smashed to smithereens. Of course my mommy blamed me. Well, all right, I admit, it looked bad. But it was all circumstantial evidence. Yes, I had been on that table with the blasted ersatz cat. And why would you have a stupid glass cat when you've got the real thing? Nonetheless, I had just been sitting there quietly reading *Cat Fancy* magazine. When I turned the page, the cat blew off the table. It just happened. Anyway, Mommy started hollering. "Cle-o!!! Cle-o!!! I swear, you're on your very last life. Tonight, you're meat loaf!"

I didn't know what to do. She really was beside herself. (What a scary thought. Mommy beside herself. Two mommies. I shudder.) Anyway, I espied Mommy's parka tossed carelessly on a chair, and I ran into the sleeve. There I sat hunkered and very quiet. Eventually, I knew the fury would pass. And she'd never think of looking for me there. I must tell you I was feeling pretty darn smug, all right. Such a clever cat am I, I thought to myself. And then someone yanked on my tail. Now, how did that happen? Yes, you guessed it. I'm ashamed to admit that I had neglected to pull my tail into the parka sleeve and my mommy had discovered me. How embarrassing is that?

Well, no harm done. I didn't end up as meat loaf. I set my purrer on overdrive, looked into my mommy's eyes with mindless adoration, and of course she melted. But how could she not?

So spill, my wonder cat. I want to know all the details of how you escaped your mommy's evil clutches.

Awed by your magnificence,

Cleo

To: CleoTheDivine@att.net

From: TyroneTheGreat@aol.com

Subject: Betrayed by a Butt

Dear Cleo, My Little Fragile Female Feline,

Caught because you let your tail hang out? Despite the double entendre, or perhaps because of it, I laughed myself absolutely stupid. I even slipped, convulsed in laughter as I was, down and off the green leather chair my mommy likes to consider her own but about which I say: he is the owner who inflicts the most tears and rips. Oh, my side hurts. Both sides hurt. And my top and bottom, too. Oh, stop, stop, this is too much.

Not that I would ever be caught in such a manner. Not me. Not ever.

Well, maybe once.

For, you see, dearest Cleo, as you wonder: where was that handsome rascal hiding? Well, I'll tell you. Do you recall that wall unit in the family room, the one with the speakers atop them? Of course you do, you poor, gentle dear. You used to climb them when you visited. And remember when you—but then, why resurrect bad memories? It was the very same wall unit that functioned as a coconspirator in my plan. If you recall, in the center of the middle of the three units, a shelf holds a large television set. And atop that set sits a long and narrow single-row CD holder.

Now, imagine if you will: the back of the television set has a slightly descending top, a sloping top that drops off at about a thirty-degree angle but is about thirty inches wide, narrowing at the back. The CD holder sits forward, leaving a small space—about four inches—at the top rear. It is, as you can imagine, warm from the set itself, and very well hidden. I managed to climb atop the wall unit and then—in the space provided as it sets away from the wall by about three inches—slip down the back of the unit onto the rear of the TV set. There I perched, very comfortable, facing forward with my paws on the shelf behind the CD holder and my body on the sloping back of the set, my rump resting up against the southeast wall of the room. Perfect, *n'est-ce pas?* Well, almost . . .

Mommy gave up on me in disgust. She began to walk back toward the front of the house and, presumably, to the truck to drive away. But I heard her stop. Imagine, again, if you will. She is passing the wall unit, and she glances to her right. She lets her gaze fall into the area between the wall unit and the wall. And what does she see? My exposed rump. My lovely black-and-white fur hanging out for all to see. How humiliating. She quickly turned on her heel, and before I had even the slightest chance to change venue, she pulled away the CD holder and we were facing each other eye to eye. And in a blink of same, she grabbed me, yanked me out, and holding me under my armpits, replaced the CD holder and stomped out of the room.

Out the front door we went, and then she opened the garage door. Why? She'd given up on me to the point she'd even put my fashionable blue prison into storage. She yanked open the door and—I swear—practically threw me into my own personal plastic hell. Then she yanked the carrier and hurled it most urgently into the back of the truck. And in another blink we were off, heading to Grandma's house. . . .

But on a happy note, I did keep Mommy occupied for very close to a full hour, building up a good head of steam and sweat, and probably working off a few pounds. You do what you can.

Sure, we were back in a few hours, but I can't begin to tell you the feeling of elation finding a new hiding place can provide. Even though I eventually let her find me (you don't think I left my ass exposed by accident, do you?), the sense of accomplishment was enormous.

Now, of course, I must find a new place for next time, and any input you might want to provide would be greatly appreciated. Since you know the place, *ma petite* . . .

I can also suggest several other places: inside file cabinets; inside mostly unused glass-enclosed shower stalls (granted, you have to jump over the top, but the exercise is good for you, and with the door firmly closed it takes hours for them to even suspect you're in there); inside the recliner-bottom hammock; inside any large speaker with a fabric cover that you can scratch open and slip into; deep into unused closets; inside any box used for Christmas decorations; and, of course, inside boxes that hold clothes Mommy has gotten too old to wear. But be careful about that last one: you could wind up at Goodwill.

Okay, this has exhausted me. It is only the hope of your visiting me again or our finding some other way to finally be alone together that sustains me. I raise a bottled-water-covered paw to you and I toast: until we share a purloined bit of double-cheese and rodent-tail pizza again, and

Avec tout mon coeur,
Tyrone the Tenacious

P.S. I'm attaching a recent photo of me for you to download. My mommy took it with her Polaroid, and I managed to make off with it before she noticed. Now that I've sent it, I'm going to lick off all the tasty film on the front. Life is good.

To: TyroneTheGreat@aol.com
From: CleoTheDivine@att.net
Subject: Haiku to You, Too

My Dearest Tyrone,

Thank you so much for the lovely photo. You look so handsome and manly wearing your tool belt. I have placed your picture near my sleeping basket, so your image is the first thing I see in the evening and the last thing I see in the morning.

I hope you enjoy the photo I'm sending you. I couldn't resist ordering the teddy from iCat's Pajamas. Don't you think it is both provocative and demure? Please do not think less of me for being so extraordinarily bold. You bring out the savage, lusty beast in me. . . . Oh, dear, I fear I'm blushing.

It's almost two o'clock in the morning as I write this. I love the night, don't you? You can get so much accomplished and without constant criticism, I might add. What I like to do is "fall asleep" on my mommy's pillow just before she goes to bed. She always says, "Oh, Cleo, sweetie, you look so innocent when you're asleep." Then she dozes. And snores. What is that, anyway? The people equivalent of purring? Or is she trying to dislodge the mother of all fur balls? Very guttural. And unattractive.

Only when I know she's sound asleep do I gently jump off the bed.

Most of all, I love to wander around those forbidden sites without Mommy screaming at me. "Cleo, get off the counter!" "Cleo, get off the dinner plate!" "Cleo, get off The Big Old Stupid Dog!" Lordy, does that woman love to hear herself talk.

First, I turn on "The Tonight Show with Jay Leno" on the off chance that it features Jay's cat, Cheese. What a hunk he is! What I find particularly endearing about this fine specimen of a feline is his ability to always best Jay. I must also compliment him on his fine manual dexterity. (Second to you, of course, dearest Ty, in both areas.) However, his paws look quite ungroomed, mangy even. You'd think with all the resources at NBC's disposal, they could avail themselves of a manicurist for Cheese. But, alas, Cheese isn't on tonight, so there is no reason to watch this show. Besides, I could do with a little snack.

I have yet to figure out how to open the big cold box. Inside I know there's chicken and some tuna salad. That would really hit the spot right now. But stare as I will, the big cold box will not open for me. The next time we see each other, perhaps you could show me how to operate a crowbar. For the nonce, I have to make do with a couple of dog treats. Dogs are so dumb they actually like these things. Don't they realize they have the taste and texture of Styrofoam? I did, however, find a box of chocolate mint Girl Scout cookies. Very tasty.

After I delicately wipe off my whiskers, I head for the office. I glance behind me and realize I've left some chocolate paw prints on the carpet. Oh, well, maybe Mommy won't notice. And so what if she does? There are two other cats that could possibly be the culprit. Maybe I can get the Big Old Stupid Dog to take the fall.

No, that won't be difficult at all. Especially with those dog treats missing.

And finally here I am in the office. Ready to work. The empty computer screen taunting me. I won't bore you with the hours of pain I spent writing these three short lines of haiku, but I will share the results with you.

PLEASING TO THE PALATE
Mouse, bird, yum yummy
Field of catnip, sea of fish
Joy to my tummy

Beautiful sentiments, *n'est-ce pas?* Haiku is difficult enough; rhyming haiku requires great mastery of the form.

Exhausted and drained from my artistic endeavor, I sink into the Barcalounger and flick on the TV with the remote. As I surf the channels, I come across an old movie. I'm a great fan of old movies, aren't you? But this one is *Rin Tin Tin.* Come on, who's going to watch a whole movie about a stupid dog? Boring, sentimental claptrap if you ask me. As Rin Tin Tin gallops clumsily across the screen, barking his stupid head off as he goes, I reflect on the love affair Hollywood has had with dogs. Not only are there the endless *Rin Tin Tin, Lassie,* and *Benji* flicks, but also we've had to endure *Beethoven I* and *II* (I was quite taken with Charles Grodin's performance in *Midnight Run.* However, now that he's associated himself with these dogs, I fear I must reevaluate his overall acting skills), *My Life as a Dog, Old Yeller, 101 Dalmatians, All Dogs Go to Heaven,* ad nauseam.

Where are the films about cats? After you mention *That Darn Cat* and its remake (making them collectively, I guess, *Those Darn*

Cats) and *Rhubarb*, the well goes pretty dry. Yes, Yes, I know cats were also featured in *Stuart Little* and *Mouse Hunt*. In the former, the felines were stereotypical villains; in the latter that pathetic cat was a victim. Totally unacceptable.

Yoo-hoo, Mr. Hollywood Producer. Just what is the all-time Broadway hit? Is it *Annie* and her stupid, vacant-eyed dog, Sandy? Or is it perchance *Cats*, which was only the longest-running Broadway show in the whole history of the whole world?

The more I think about it, the angrier I become. Am I missing an entire oeuvre of feline flicks? Uh-oh, I hear Mommy stirring. I'd better go find some innocent little diversion to pacify her. I know, I know. I'll curl up in the basket on top of the fridge. The one with all the potatoes in it. Mommy thinks I look especially cute there. And indeed I do, my chartreuse eyes peering out from between the spuds.

If you think of other cat pix, please let me know. You know, now that I think about it, wouldn't you and I be a fabulous movie couple? Better than Lombard and Gable. Better than Hepburn and Tracy. Better than Bacall and Bogie. Cleo and Tyrone! Our very names sound like film royalty.

That's all, felines!

Cleo

To: CleoTheDivine@att.net
From: TyroneTheGreat@aol.com
Subject: Haiku, Part Deux

Dear Miss Cleo, My Lithe and Lean Lady,
Wow, wow, meow, meow, you really are the cat's pajamas, or the cat's meow, depending on your decade of reference. And pink-and-black lace, no less! Is that a bit of drool on the screen and keyboard? No matter. More pictures, please. If we can't be together, at least I can print them out and paste them up inside my litter box and think of you each and every time . . . Well, you know.

Loved the poem. I've been working on a bit of haiku myself. Try this one on:

VOMIT ON THE CARPET
Brown, sticky, gummy,
Gross and vile, stinky, lumpy.
Clean it up, Mummy!

Anyway, it's just a rough draft. I've got to get an editor on it. Or a thesaurus. Whatever.

But you, my pet, are the true writer between us. And, speaking of that and of your oh-so-true complaints about the lack of decent thought-provoking films for those of the feline persuasion, I ask you: why don't you write one yourself? Put those dainty little paws to keyboard and do it!

Well, with that I must offer a hasty adieu. I have just heard the sound of a can opening, and I can't be left behind in what has come to resemble the Oklahoma land rush segment of *Far and Away* around here.

All my love, you little bee's knees,

Tyrone the Tantalizer

To: TyroneTheGreat@aol.com

From: CleoTheDivine@att.net

Subject: *Revolting Cats*, A Screenplay

My Precious, Polka-dotted Poet,

Your poem is genius personified. What realism! What grittiness! What texture! I've never seen Haiku Noir executed with such aplomb.

As a result of your most excellent suggestion, I have indeed tried my paw at writing a screenplay. I don't know why everyone makes such a big deal about it, because I found it flowed right out of me. But then, I am a natural-born writer, so maybe it just comes more easily to me. Whatever.

I propose the following sweeping multigenerational saga. I call it simply *Revolting Cats*.

Ext. Catnip Fields — Daybreak

ANGLE ON the sun as it peeks over the horizon, slowly filling our field of vision. It is large. It is orange. It fills your heart with optimism. It signals the start of a new day, of a new beginning. CAMERA ANGLES DOWN to a field of catnip extending as far as the eye can see. CAMERA SLOWLY ZOOMS FORWARD to reveal four cats, working the fields. JENNY is only a year old, but the punishing fields make her appear much older. Hard already. Abandoned as a mere kitten, she was sold into slavery before she was even weaned. There's JOSE, who has been working the fields for years. He no longer has dreams and aspirations. He's old now, waiting and hoping for death to release him. Beside him works his eldest daughter, MONICA. Oh, she was a happy cat once. She was in love with Rick, who left her the moment she told him she was pregnant. Raising her babies alone, working all her life in the fields has left her a bitter, unfulfilled woman. All their little paws are bloody and callous from picking the catnip; the soles of their paws are thin; and their coats aren't nearly thick enough to ward off the cold mornings. And they're all in desperate need of dental care. And some grooming. Whenever they slow down, just to wipe the blood off their tiny paws, the evil overseer, SPOT, a dog (of course), cracks his whip, yells at them to keep working. The one cat who will not be bullied by Spot is CHAD, who remains unbowed, proud. Handsome, idealistic, Chad has risen above his own humble but loving beginnings to assume a leadership position. Kind, gentle, and generous, he urges and encourages his fellow felines to always keep their spirits up, their dignity intact. It will be Chad who will strengthen their resolve to find a better life.

And then the cats escape the yoke of their oppression.

And then they take over the world.

And then Chad becomes king.

And then all the dogs are banished to Barstow.

THE END

Since I am an artiste, I don't have a head for business, so perhaps I should consider an agent to help me with those dreary, tiresome details.

In drafting my contract, I will of course include clauses about points, domestic sales to TV (both network and cable), videocassette compensation, electronic media, foreign distribution, merchandising royalties, credit (mine above the title, of course). And I have very definite brilliant ideas about casting, directors, makeup and hair, marketing strategies, promotion and publicity (what could possibly be better than me appearing on TV screens across the country promoting the film, à la Danielle Steel?).

Oops! Mommy just brought out the dreaded vacuum cleaner. That thing's so powerful it could suck out your soul, I swear. I once got my tail caught in it, and . . . Well, it's a long, boring, unattractive story. Suffice it to say it wasn't a pleasant experience, I can tell you that. Well, time for *moi* to hang out on the top closet shelf, far away from that death machine.

While hiding out in the closet, I'm going to try to devise a plan where we can see each other. Hmmm . . . Let me think, let me think. . . . Surely I can come up with something. . . .

A bientôt, mon cher,
Cleo

To: CleoTheDivine@att.net
From: TyroneTheGreat@aol.com
Subject: LizzieBeth and Magic Marker

Most Excellent Cleo, Princess of Pets,

Not much time here, so I'll just dash off a note to let you know I'm okay and thinking of you. And, of course, a moment of silence in honor of your script. Such passion! Such drama! It would sweep the Oscars in many, many CATegories. And who to play you (yes, disguised as Monica, but still you, my lovely), none other than Julie Newmar. A much younger Julie Newmar, of course, but they can do so much with computers these days. And as for Chad (who, dare I say it, bears more than a slight resemblance to *moi*), none other than Tom "the Cat" Cruise. Type on, my sensitive scenarist, for soon the world will be yours.

But as for my world, busy, busy, busy—so much to do, so little time. First, there was the business with Mommy's purse, the black leather one. You know it, large and misshapen, red interior, long black strap? Probably so old it could vote. I've tried to explain to her on more than one occasion that she really needed to find and purchase a new one, something more fashionable and au courant, if you know what I mean? But does she listen to me? No. So today, as I was taking a short snooze on the kitchen table, the aforementioned purse nearby, I opened one eye to watch LizzieBeth jump onto the counter. I remained very still, and she knew not I was even there. I waited. First, LizzieBeth approached the toaster, about which she holds definite opinions. Something to do with a singed tail. I don't recall. And then she leapt upon it and peed inside. She really did. Then she glanced around, looking from one side to the other, and satisfied the coast was clear, she jumped onto the open purse and peed into it, too. A good, long, smelly pee. I could not believe it. What was this all about? She offered no explanation. And then she jumped off the counter and disappeared. What was I to do? I knew when Mommy noticed what LizzieBeth had done, there would be big trouble in River City. Should I tell her? Point it out? No, she might think it was me, though I've never done anything like that in my life. No, I'd best just lay low. I'll get up and go into the bedroom and sleep a while in the closet ironing basket. But no, I waited too long, and there she was. Maybe she only came in for a cup of coffee. No such luck. Mommy headed straight for the purse. She reached in and—she shrieked in a manner and volume I'd never heard before. She screamed and ranted and raved and turned the purse upside down onto the kitchen table. Hey, wait a minute! I'm sleeping here! Then she finally calmed herself and began to wash everything down. By the way, to no avail. The purse and its contents still stink. Time for a new purse, you think?

As she went on and on and on about the purse, not even noticing me in her anger, I went to the toy box. Now, as I've mentioned before, I really like the toy box. It's only cardboard, but it has lots and lots of good stuff in it. I suddenly realized that both Magic and LizzieBeth were also availing themselves of toys in the box. Now, that will not do. Did they not realize I had laid claim to that box? Apparently not. So, taking my cue from the ever-moist LizzieBeth, I peed in it. Not once, but three times. That should make possession clear.

Then it was on to the drapes, five pair in all, all white and all in dire need of a drop or two of identification fluid, enough so that I could eradicate Magic's scent, which he drops everywhere, if you know what I mean. Then a bit here and there, on the recliner in the bedroom, the ottoman in the TV room, on the blinds in the office . . . You get the idea. I am weak with dehydration.

In other words, Cleo my love, it's a great deal of work to live here. For, as soon as I spray out my calling card, which I have had to do only since that interloper Magic came to live with us, Mommy, clearly exhibiting signs of obsessive-compulsive syndrome, cleans up after me, completely neutralizing my lovely scent and replacing it with something called eau de Clorox.

I don't think so. . . .

What do you do about that? Or is this, as has been suggested, a "male" thing? I don't know about you, but if my scent isn't everywhere, I begin to feel distinctly dislocated. Maybe it's just me.

So write me soon. I dream of the day our paws can touch once again, your pure white fur on mine—sharing together a pungent dead bird or crème de tail of rat hollandaise. But right now what I really need is a long, cool drink of toilet water. That right-after-the-flush stuff is just *magnifique!* So to the bathroom I go, hanging around, waiting for the diet cola to do its work on Mommy's plumbing. And then she can return the favor.

Until then, all my love,

Tyrone the Tartar

Dearest Tyrone,

What a clever puss to recognize you were the prototype for Chad, the most perfect cat in the whole entire world. You are he, my buffed hero.

Now, about that "marking" business. I do think that's a guy thing. For *moi*, I prefer tasteful monograms. *Mais*, as they say, *chacun à son goût*.

If only I had followed my horoscope's advice today. It clearly suggested this was not going to be a banner day for *moi*. It indicated serious health problems, an interloper taking over, and no albacore tuna today. I guffawed. I really did. No day could be that bad.

But my stars! No sooner did I read those ominous words when I suddenly doubled over in pain. My little tummy ached. I collapsed onto the sofa, feeling pale, wan, and shocky. I put my little paw to my forehead and looked pained. I began to cry piteously. You know that cry you get when you have a urinary tract infection? Yes, that cry. It makes Mommy come running every single time.

She cuddled me in her arms and spoke baby talk to me. How embarrassing is that? My daddy came over and looked at me and said, "She's bloated. She's probably constipated." Oh puhleeze, if I'm going to feel this terrible, there's going to be something a little more wrong with me than constipation, I can assure you.

And then you know what he did? I still can't believe it. He picked me up, lifted my tail—oh, this is so embarrassing—and he looked at my . . . my . . . okay, let's call it my derrière and be done with it.

"Yes," Daddy said. "She's constipated." He took me into the bathroom and put Vaseline on my . . . my . . . my . . . tush. I've never been so mortified in my life.

Nothing happened, and I continued to howl in that piteous fashion. My tummy really did hurt. I felt like I had swallowed a molten bowling ball. It's probably an ulcer, I thought. Stress has obviously finally caught up with me. And who wouldn't get an ulcer if they had to live with the same stress as *moi?* Mafia cats, mommies and daddies who leave me alone for hours at a time, a career that might be passing me by just because I'm six (it doesn't seem to matter that I can still fit perfectly into my senior prom gown). Now, let me think. How do they treat an ulcer? Oh yeah, I remember. Milk, cheese, ice cream. Well, how bad can that be?

Mommy and Daddy continued to monitor my every move—as it were—checking the litter box and my . . . my . . . my . . . bottom constantly. There was a lot of whispered conversation between

Mommy and Daddy. I could tell Daddy was not very happy. "Why does that darn cat always wait until Sunday night at eleven o'clock to get sick? That means we're going to have to take her to the Really Outrageously Expensive Emergency Animal Hospital." What a funny name for a hospital, I thought. I shrugged. Oh well, truth in advertising.

Daddy threw me in my carrier, and none too gently I might add. You'd think he'd be a little more careful with someone who is already in so much pain. On the drive to the animal hospital, Daddy lectured me. He is usually a pretty mellow, quiet guy, but when he gets wound up about something, Lordy, how he can carry on. "You know what your problem is, Cleo? You eat plastic bags. Plastic bags do not constitute one of the major food groups. In fact, they are indigestible. Do you have any idea how much this is going to set me back?"

Yeah, yeah, yeah, I thought. Most models have a cocaine habit, and this guy is complaining about plastic bags. Get a grip, Daddy. Time for a reality check.

When we arrived at the Really Outrageously Expensive Emergency Animal Hospital, I was surprised to see several other ailing animals ahead of me. I heard a Persian's mommy tell the lady at the desk that Fluffy (oh, puhleez!) seemed depressed, angry, and cranky. Excuse me, lady, if I had a pushed-in face like Fluffy's, I'd be depressed, angry, and cranky, too. Then my daddy got to the check-in desk and announced in a loud stentorian voice that his stupid cat was constipated. Hey, buddy, could you say it a little louder? I don't think the folks in Ames, Iowa, heard you.

We were put into a little tiny exam room, and I was instructed to sit on the metal table. Do you know how cold that felt on my bottom? Not good at all. The doctor came in, reading my chart. He picked me up and—are you ready for this?—he lifted my tail and looked at my . . . my . . . my . . . butt!

"Yep," he said. "She's constipated, all right. We'll have to give her an enema." He told Daddy to come back in a couple of hours. After they had flushed me out. Whatever that means.

I don't know if you've ever had one of these, Tyrone, but if you ever even hear the word, do whatever you have to do to escape. I won't describe the actual mechanics of the procedure, but I will say it's extremely gross and indelicate. It left me with the worst case of diarrhea I've ever had. And this is their miracle cure?! This doctoring business has a long way to go.

When Daddy came back for me, the doctor said he wanted him to add Metamucil to my cat food and also a pumpkin. I imagine Metamucil is the brand name for the most expensive white albacore tuna. The pumpkin part confused me for a moment. Then I remembered how I enjoyed the jack-o'-lantern Daddy carved out of a pumpkin. I especially loved it when he cut himself. How he did howl! I laughed myself silly, I can tell you. Probably the doctor prescribed the pumpkin for my emotional well-being; he knew that a jack-o'-lantern would lift my spirits.

Well, as it turns out, Metamucil is NOT a fancy brand of tuna. It's difficult to describe, but if you will imagine sprinkling kitty litter over your wet food—Day-Glo orange kitty litter to boot— you'll have a close approximation of how this stuff tastes. And the pumpkin was not made into a comical jack-o'-lantern. Instead, I was supposed to eat this. Now, I ask you, in the wilds, do felines eat Metamucil and pumpkins? I think not.

Well, *cher ami*, please take care of yourself. I think we've learned a few valuable lessons here: (1) Metamucil is not tuna; (2) don't eat plastic bags; (3) be very afraid if someone even mentions the word *enema*.

Avec tout mon amour,

Cleo

To: CleoTheDivine@att.net

From: TyroneTheGreat@aol.com

Subject: *Plus Ça Change, Plus C'est La Même Chose*

My Dearest Cleo,

Ah, ma petite, I was devastated to learn of your latest medical adventure. Delicately put, it sounds really, really gross. But at least you got to go to the Really Outrageously Expensive Emergency Animal Hospital. Like I always say, if the mommies make us sick, the very least they must do is pay for it. So you're okay now, yes? And fully up to snuff? You'd better be, 'cause I've got important, and very serious, news.

Let us review: We live (or lived, as it will soon become apparent) in this rather oversized abode atop the hill. The location, far and away from everything, had its good points: a long ride to the vet's, lots of birds upon which to gawk and therefore stalk, and so on. The bad points: coyotes. Dozens, perhaps even millions, of them. These brazen, mangy creatures even had the audacity to come up on our deck and gaze at us in our playroom (i.e., the entire house) via the French doors. I can hear their tiny little brains now: kitty *à l'orange*, Kentucky Fried Kitty, a Big McCat, etc. *Dégoûtante.*

Anyway, Mommy has recently been complaining about running up and down the hill in that baby-size truck of hers. What an embarrassment that vehicle is. A Trooper, I could see. A Blazer, even. A Land Cruiser or Humvee would be best, but I could even accept a Mercedes SUV. This little four-cylinder bright-red excuse for a four-wheel drive? Please. She even has to turn off the air conditioner and the radio to make it up the hill. But I digress. She also griped about being so far from everything and the cost of maintaining a huge house, etc., etc., etc., as if I didn't hold up my end at all. Who does she think yanks down all that toilet paper for her off the roll so she can ball it up and wipe down the toilet area? (Granted, from the water I splash from the bowl, but are we getting picky or what?)

So, suddenly our house was filled with empty boxes. Dozens, maybe even thousands, of them. And bit by bit, items began to disappear. Into the boxes, I presumed. And then the boxes would be taped shut and removed from the house.

Each and every morning I would arise to discover yet more items missing. I would frantically race into the kitchen and find only a modicum of comfort to discover that my water bowl and food dish were still on the eating rug, but it was but a modicum.

Curtains and drapes came down and disappeared; rugs vanished; whole pieces of furniture (the entire office comes to mind!) just up and turned to dust! (Which explains, if not excuses, the fact I haven't written for so very long. The entire computer, fax, printer disappeared. What was I to do? It's not as if I'm any good at cursive writing, you know. It's this paw thing. . . .)

Not only that, but soon Mommy herself began to disappear for long periods of time during the day, only to return dirty and tired. She would feed us first thing (thank goodness she did not shirk her responsibilities due to vague excuses such as exhaustion or whatever) and then collapse into a deep sleep from which she would not arise until the next morning, no matter how much I harassed her.

And for what, I ask you. Imagine this: The old place was a box of sorts. It was divided into smaller boxes by things called "walls." The walls were all painted white, the floors were all covered with a sort of mauve-beige carpet, with the exception of the bathrooms and the kitchen, upon which some sort of smooth covering was upon the floor. There were windows consisting of small panes of glass, and all the rooms were filled with furniture, decorative items (not all in the best of taste, but they seemed to appeal to Mommy for some strange reason), clothes, food, dishes, etc. In effect, the usual. So what happens? Mommy supervises the removal from our home, the only home I have ever known, I repeat, of everything. Yes, everything. All that is left is us. In carriers. And then even we are removed. And where do we end up? Now, get this.

It is a large box, divided into smaller boxes by "walls." The number of smaller boxes appears to be roughly the same as before, if you don't count those areas in the old place that were always "off limits." The walls are white, and the carpets are mauve-beige. Except for the kitchen and bathrooms, upon which some sort of smooth covering exists. And all the rooms are filled up with exactly the same furniture and decorations that were in the old house. And in the exact same configuration! Now, I ask you: does this make any sense? Even the windows are the same, all with screens keeping us in even when the windows are open.

People have pieces missing. First, would a proper feline ever do such a thing? No. When we leave, we leave everything behind. If one is to make a proper new start, why encumber oneself with old furniture and dishes? No, we simply hit the road and start anew. We are, in fact, the Kerouacs of the nonhuman world. Second, and let's face it, this is the important item here: we would NEVER LEAVE in the first place. Why? Oh, sure, sure, I can understand taking off in a fit of pique or retaliation for our mommy's switching to discount cat food, but just for the sake of leaving? No. We need a good reason, a life-changing reason, or we stay put. Period.

But there is good news. I happened to take notice of Mommy's name, address, and date book (it is, sadly, so often empty. She leads such a dull life, poor thing. I suggested pottery or rock collecting, but does she listen?) and discovered that my new home is not very far from you. In fact, I heard my mommy say she is about to switch all of us to the same vet you go to. Is he or she any good? I hate changing vets without a proper recommendation.

Okay, so things seem under control. Or seemed. Just this morning, what do I see? Mommy's suitcases. The good Lark suitcases. Out on the bedroom floor.

Uh-oh . . .

With much love, fear, and trepidation,

Tyrone the Temblor

To: TyroneTheGreat@aol.com
From: CleoTheDivine@att.net
Subject: Moving, Metamucil, and Mengele, Oh, My . . .

Tyrone, *Mon Cher,*

Thank you for commiserating with me about my recent malady. Rest assured I am fine, but it goes without saying I'm languishing around the house for my mommy's benefit. I find if I do the Debra Winger thing from *Terms of Endearment,* I get a whole lot more attention and lap time. I even turned my delicate mauve nose up at albacore tuna yesterday. It was a huge sacrifice, but on the other hand, it made my mommy crazy. She was convinced I was near death's door. She held me for hours, even covering me with my favorite quilt. I figure I can milk this for at least another two weeks.

As for the Metamucil and pumpkin, Mommy can just forget about that. Do you know she even tried to sprinkle Metamucil on my tuna? First of all, as I mentioned, it's bright orange. Did she think I wouldn't notice? Hey, lady, give me a little credit here. We have reached a détente of sorts: she dutifully puts a discreet helping of pumpkin on my plate and just as dutifully I gingerly eat around it.

Your move does indeed seem absolutely senseless. I certainly think there are legitimate reasons for relocating. I just assumed that your mommy had found a property that included a catnip field, a pond stocked with trout, halibut, and salmon (no catfish, please!), a reptile house filled with salamanders and lizards, and a pen for small free-range rodents. But you didn't mention any of these amenities, so I truly am confused as to the point of this move. What could your mommy have been thinking? By the way, did she pack the Weedwacker, too? Did she really bring that Weapon of Mass Destruction to your new abode? I really think you must consider the possibility that your mommy has some psychotic tendencies that you simply choose to ignore.

You asked for a recommendation for my vet. The man I call Mengele? The man who eats fava beans and enjoys a good chianti? No, I fear he is not to be recommended; he is to be avoided. And if this is not possible—due to persuasive, bullying mommies and dreaded blue carriers—then he is, alas, to be endured. Here's a little tip, however. This angel of death has a beard. I like to swat at it. Back and forth I go. Whack, whack, whack. Sometimes, my delicate little paw "gets caught" in this unsightly facial fuzz, and in an attempt to disengage my paw, I "accidentally" scratch him. Oops!

It beats the heck outta me why your mommy has the good luggage on the floor. Is it, I hope, just a sign of her sloth?
Forever yours,
Cleo

To: CleoTheDivine@att.net
From: TyroneTheGreat@aol.com
Subject: Byron, Shelley, Keats, and Me

My Dearest Cleo,

Alas, I suspect the removal of the suitcases from their home at the top of the closet is not simply sloth, as you logically suggested, but something far more sinister. For, upon closer examination of our dwelling, such as it is, I discovered something else: Mommy's clothes in plastic bags. On hangers. Hanging on that funny contraption that hooks over the bedroom door and from which I like to swing from time to time. While at first you might respond "Yummy!" knowing as I do your penchant for the ever-edible plastic, I think—upon further examination—you, too, will have to agree: something is afoot. Or apaw, as I prefer it. Those bags with her clothing within only appear after I have taken the liberty of moistening a particular item of clothing with my scent, so Mommy will not forget me in her occasional absences. Or when I have deposited a particularly impressive furball onto a sweater or pair of slacks. Or when I decided dry cat food really doesn't agree with me and allow it all to escape my digestive system via mouth and onto her newest suit. But, alas, I have participated in none of those activities, and yet the clothes in the plastic bags have reappeared. What could it mean? Thinking about it makes my brain hurt. I think I'll play with my catnip ball. And forward to you one of my latest creations.

I have taken time from my incredibly busy schedule to compose, in your honor, a new poem. Ah-hem.

ODE TO CLEO
(Aka Eau de Cleo)
How my heart sings
and my feet pitter-patter
whenever I hear or think
of how you nag and natter
oh, my Cleo
my friend-o
my Cleo

Away we will go
together
Cleo

When things are real bad
I never get mad
I think of my Cleo
and feel really neat-o
'cause my pretty Cleo
is all that I need-o
to feel just fine
Cleo, my divine

Away we will go
together
Cleo

So whenever you're down
and I'm not to be found
don't frown or get blue
just know I love you
my Cleo
my Cleo
my very best friend-o

My confidante and pal
you're the very best gal
whether feather or fur
loving you's de rigueur
my Cleo petite
with tiny white feet

I love you Cleo
you're my very best friend-o
Cleo, Cleo, Cleo

The End.

Okay, so maybe it's not Paul Simon, but the thought is there.
Oh, Cleo, I miss you!
Love,
Tyrone the Tiger

To: TyroneTheGreat@aol.com
FROM: CleoTheDivine@att.net
SUBJECT: *La Bohème, à La Chat*

My Sweet, Dearest Tyrone,

I'm incredibly touched by your poetic offering. The sentiments expressed were so pure and honest they brought tears to my beautiful chartreuse eyes. I have wrapped the poem in lavender ribbon and dried catnip and placed it in my hope chest (and you know what I'm hoping, don't you?).

I have, of course, memorized the entire poem, and every morning, just before I nod off, I recite it over and over again—my own personal mantra:

> oh, my Cleo
> my friend-o
> my Cleo

Seemingly so simple but bursting with subtext and raw emotion. And my name is filled with music, *n'est-ce pas?* A veritable symphony. This is an excellent example of the difficult-to-execute rhyming scheme called catterel, is it not? You have created an amazing piece of work, but I would expect nothing less from you, my pinto Lord Byron!

I've been bursting with news to share with you. Guess what? Stealth has run away from home! I must admit I helped him a little in his decision to seek greener pastures. At first I tried to encourage him with words like "Unless you take drastic steps, you're going to be caged like this for the rest of your whole life" and "Gee, isn't this the night you and your cronies usually go out for a friendly game of poker? Don't you miss your buddies?" But Stealth isn't a cat of words. No, I had to take a more direct approach with him. What I finally did was place a little hammer and other appropriate tools near the window screen. Eventually, he got the idea (I never said this was a smart cat!) and made his escape.

Mommy was, of course, very sad, boo-hooing all over the place. She searched the neighborhood hourly, made a huge pest of herself at the animal shelter, and tacked up tacky notices about the missing feline all over the place. Poor Mommy! Poor Stealth! Who cares?

But alas, this silver cloud has a black crepe paper lining. The thug cat came back. One morning Mommy went out to get the paper and he was sitting there big as life. Mommy scooped him up in her arms, carried him all over the house, telling him—in that really sickening voice—how much she missed him and how much she loved him. She promised that he would be the one cat in the menagerie who would be allowed both indoor and outdoor privileges because he was so special. I'm telling you, it's enough to make one puke.

Or in my case, caused me to break out in a really nasty rash. My delicate little ears, my toes, the bottoms of my paws, even my face are covered with runny little sores. Very *dégoûtante!* And there was the constant worry that I would scar. Then, what would happen to my modeling career?

I completely lost my appetite, too. I felt so weak, wan, and pale. You know how Mimi felt at the end of *La Bohème*? That's exactly how I felt. Well, she died and I didn't, but you get the idea.

Would Mommy let me lick my wounds in peace? Of course not. No, she had to stuff me into one of those foul-smelling carriers and haul me to the vet's again.

As we waited for the doctor, my mommy babbled on and on that my illnesses—real and imagined—always cost her an arm and a leg. I glanced over and saw that all of her limbs were present and accounted for, so I don't know what she's blathering on about. She said with all the money she'd spent on me here, I probably paid for one of the exam rooms single-pawedly. Well, if one of these exam rooms is mine, I want my pictures plastered all over the wall. I'll have to remember to send some eight-by-ten glossies and some paw prints.

The doctor examined me—and none too gently, I might add. He said he wanted to check for fleas and ticks. I beg your pardon! *Moi!* Ticks! Those two words (*Cleo* and *ticks*) do not belong in the same sentence. Nope, he explained after putting a piece of my delicate skin under his microscope, no ticks. He decided I was having an allergic reaction of some sort. Of course, he didn't have a clue what I might be allergic to. Some help, huh? This doctoring business doesn't seem like a very exact science, does it?

If you want my opinion, my delicate condition is caused by stress. Who wouldn't be stressed by all the fuss everyone made about that darn thug cat? Do you know Mommy even made a special trip to the pet store to buy that mange machine a welcome home catnip toy? I simply can't allow myself to dwell on this. I can feel hives starting to break out on my forehead....

And if all this isn't enough stress, I'm very concerned about what's going on at your home. I think it's very ominous indeed that your mommy's luggage and clothes in plastic bags are scattered about your house. Is your mommy going somewhere? And what's to become of you? Is she going to leave you there alone to fend for yourself? She wouldn't be that cruel. Wait a minute.... Wait a minute.... Remember when my mommy and daddy went away skiing or snorkeling or whatever the hell they were doing? What did they do with me and my siblings? They brought us to your house! Is it possible your mommy's going to bring you to my house? We'll have such fun. You've never been to my place, but I think you'll appreciate my decorating efforts. There are oodles and oodles of nifty hidey holes where we can hang out. Think of the fun we could have. Playing mind games on the dog, though admittedly it's not much of a challenge. And maybe we could begin a subtle but effective *Gaslight*ing campaign on Stealth. Just think, Tyrone, very soon we could be wrapped in each other's paws. I can't wait.

You must check your mommy's appointment book for any additional clues. I'll do the same. Maybe there's an entry in Mommy's book about cats coming to visit. I can't wait! I can't wait! I can't wait!

With all my love,

Cleo

To: CleoTheDivine@att.net
FROM: TyroneTheGreat@aol.com
SUBJECT: *Qu'est-ce que c'est* "Kamp Kritter"?

My Lovely Cleo,

Well, I checked my mommy's appointment book. Nothing. I went right to the end of the year, for heaven's sake, and not a thing. But then she's not always meticulous about her entries.

Okay, so then I checked the mail on the off chance there's any correspondence between your mommy and my mommy. All right, all right: I purloined the mail. I waited until I heard the mail person drop off all that neat paper stuff (have you ever tasted the glue they use on the Publishers Clearing House mailing? Simply wonderful), snatched it away and ran with it, all stuffed in my mouth, into the office. I do suspect Mommy's on to me, however. I overheard her on the phone complain to someone that all her mail seems to be covered with a thick coat of fish-scented saliva. Although, for the life of me, I would think that would be an improvement, but what do I know?

And, lo and behold, I discovered one of those simperingly cute postcards from some joint called Kamp Kritter. You know the type: a sketch on one side of a kitten and a puppy frolicking or

111

sleeping together? Oh, puhleeze . . . As if any self-respecting cat would do that. No wonder they used a sketch. No photograph has ever been nor ever will be available without an assist from computer enhancement. Anyway, on this postcard the names listed as the "guests," scheduled for arrival on August 11 and departure on August 15, are—you guessed it!—LizzieBeth, Magic, me, and Lucy the Dog!

Now, enlighten me, O all-knowing Cleo: what the hell is Kamp Kritter? Sounds like a place for gay dogs, if you know what I mean. "Oh, Chester, simply love the spots. But if I were you, I'd lose the twelve-pound fatty tumor on your leg." That sort of thing.

I'll keep you updated. Hope you're feeling better. And you'd better not have anything infectious. Though catching anything from you wouldn't be all that terrible.

Much love,

Tyrone the Two-Tone

To: TyroneTheGreat@aol.com
From: CleoTheDivine@att.net
Subject: Cleo the Divine, Private Investigator

My Handsome Stud Muffin,

Kamp Kritter?! You and your kin are going to Kamp Kritter?!
Kamp Kritter (isn't that inkredibly kute?!) is attached to Mengele's veterinary practice. "Kamp" denotes either a resort setting with spas, massages, sparkling pools, and long, cool drinks with tiny, brightly colored umbrellas. Or, perhaps, in the more rustic sense, it denotes tents, roasting hot dogs and marshmallows on a stick over a campfire, and singing rousing drinking songs under star-filled unpolluted skies. Kamp Kritter resembles none of the above. Think a cage. For long periods of time. And there are dogs there. Lots of barking dogs.

But why in heaven would your mommy send you guys there when she could simply drop you over at my place? Unless . . . Unless . . . Oh, I just had a thought. A horrible thought. Let me do some sleuthing and get back to you.

Keep your handsome, manly toes crossed. If my suspicions

are correct, no, I won't even articulate it. It's too horrible to contemplate.

Hoping the cat gods are with us!

Cleo

Dear Dr. Mengele,

I swear I'm on my last brain cell. For the life of me I can't remember if I made reservations for Cleo, Honey, Stealth, and the Big Old Stupid Dog for August 11–15.

Could you confirm their reservations for me? Did I by chance also give you a contact number in case of emergency?

By the way, if I booked a teeth cleaning for their stay, I'd like to cancel that. Well, keep the appointment for the Big Old Stupid Dog and Stealth. Cleo and Honey should have a manicure and pedicure only.

And I'd like to request the corner suite for Cleo. And please don't forget that she particularly favors fish-neck stew and mouse ears en brochette.

Sincerely,

Mommy Hamner

To: LindaHamner@att.net
From: SkipMengleDVM@KampKritter.com
Subject: Reservations

Dear "Mommy" Hamner,

Indeed you did make reservations for the kids on August 11–
15. I'm sorry, but I'll be unable to accommodate your request for
the corner suite for Cleo. The Taco Bell Chihuahua has booked
that suite for those same days.

I've checked Cleo's and Honey's files, and they're long over-
due for their teeth cleaning. I think we should try to fit them in.
If anything, I think they could go without their manicure/pedicure
on this visit.

Indeed you did leave us your contact number. The Plaza in
New York. Nice going!

And tell Cleo she'll eat gruel like the rest of our "guests." I
swear, that cat needs to get over herself. By the way, how is her
constipation problem? Is she still full of shit?

Check-in time is 11:30 A.M.

I hope you and Ms. Browne have a wonderful time in the Big

Apple. Good luck with your publisher. I'm anxious to meet Virginia's crew.

Regards,

Skip Mengele, DVM

To: TyroneTheGreat@aol.com
From: CleoTheDivine@att.net
Subject: *En Vacances*

My Dearest Tyrone,

The worst possible news! Through an enormously clever subterfuge on my part, I have discovered that my mommy is sending us to Kamp Kritter, too. And get this! Your mommy and my mommy are going to New York together! And leaving us in that dreadful hellhole called Kamp Kritter.

I can't believe they're not taking us to New York. It's only the height of the fashion season, for cat's sakes. Doesn't Mommy think I'd like to see this year's crop of supermodels taking their stroll down the catwalk? I'm not even bitter that it could have been me up there if it weren't for that limp caused by the nasty fall off your bookcase and that pesky skin condition. I've discovered if I wear a black veil, hardly anyone notices the rash, and the veil adds a certain air of mystery. Someone did, however, mistake me for a beekeeper, but that, I think, was an aberration.

Can you imagine the two of us in New York, Tyrone? Taking a stroll, paw in paw, through Central Park, pausing along the way to eviscerate a bird or squirrel, going down to South Street Seaport for a visit to Fulton Fish Market, and taking in a matinee of *The Lion King.* How romantic that would have been!

But no, we're going to Kamp Kritter. It's so incredibly unfair. After all I've done for that woman . . . Wait a minute! Time out here! When life hands you a lemon, have a glass of champagne (not domestic, of course). Tyrone, here I was thinking this was the worst possible news. But as it turns out, it's the best possible news ever! We're going to be at Mengele's Kamp Kritter at exactly the same time! Together! You and I! Yes, I would have preferred our romantic rendezvous to have taken place on the Côte d'Azur, but with our transcendental love and our incredible beauty, we will transform those dreary digs into a romantic wonderland!

Already I'm atwitter. There's so much we can do! Read poetry to each other, play catnasta, watch some kitty videos, play mind games with the dogs. And then when the owners come to pick them up, their precious pooches will be reduced to drooling, slack-jawed psychological meltdowns. Oh, that pretty much describes dogs in their normal condition, doesn't it? Oh, well, we'll still have plenty of laughs over that, I can tell you.

The food there is from hunger, however. They pretty much serve gruel. Gruel for breakfast, gruel for lunch, well, you get the idea. Personally, I think we should bring in our own comestibles. By the way, has your mommy bought you that new sliced chicken in gravy? Quite tasty. And if worse comes to worst, there's a pizza boîte down the street from Kamp, and we can order in an anchovy pizza.

I'm suddenly very jazzed, and I can't wait to start packing. I ordered a new negligee through iCat's Pajamas. Don't blush, big guy, but I had you in mind when I purchased it. Also, I have a new bottle of Eau de Rodent, which is considered quite the aphrodisiac.

Until we are cuddled in each other's arms,

Cleo

To: CleoTheDivine@att.net
From: TyroneTheGreat@aol.com
Subject: An *Animal House* Vacation

My Little Cabbage Cleo,

Leave it to you to make champagne from lemons, and bitter, shriveled ones at that, to turn catastrophe into opportunity! Yes, yes, I see what you have in mind.

We will meet in the waiting room of Mengele's Animal Hospital and Kamp Kritter, each of us in our respective carriers, facing each other, so near and yet so far. Each of us will extend through the prison of our wire grates one of our delicately groomed paws, and in that electric moment, our fur and claws will touch, and it will be magic!

You will groom, won't you? I hate it when all that loose nail gunk is hanging off the claws and the edges are rough. Did you know, by the way, that there are far too many mommies who have their feline companion's claws REMOVED?! It's true, it's true: I saw it on *Hard Copy.* Our feline brethren (and sisteren, I guess) are put out on the surgical table, and then their claws are cut out. (Now, now, Cleo, don't get squeamish on me. This is information you must know in order to protect yourself in the future. Remember the spinning wheel and all that.) It's as if a human had their fingers removed at the first knuckle. It's absolutely barbaric.

And for what must we endure this? So their stupid furniture will remain pristine, for God's sake. Furniture? Drapes? Oh, puhleez . . . In this life, one has to make a choice: good furniture in perfect repair or the absolutely delightful and irreplaceable company of the feline persuasion. There is no middle ground. Declawing indeed!

Oh, but I did get off on another rant, didn't I? Well, back to the issue at hand: Kamp Kritter.

You don't think they'll try to keep us separated, do you? Sort of like putting the males and females in separate rooms as in youth hostels? I don't think I could bear that. So let's think positively: we will be together. For a whole five days at Kamp Kritter. What to pack, what to pack . . .

For starters, a warm, snuggly blanket is a must. Two is even better. Some catnip, preferably in a burlap sack, all the better for sucking on, you know. A copy of the feline edition of Trivial Pursuit; a roll of toilet paper for shredding, should things get dull; a small battery-operated sound-effects key chain (the car horn sound is especially frightening to dogs, who appear to be affected by things like that, and so most amusing to those of us immune to idle threats); a sleep mask (in those kennels, they often leave the lights on at night, as if it were a gulag or such); and of course our own edibles, along with a chef, if possible. Oh, rats, I forgot: our chefs are going to New York. Scratch that. Ha-ha. In-joke for cats.

What else? A dirty sock is always fun, and string of any length. I also tend to enjoy a good game of drench-the-sable-end-with-saliva, using Mommy's makeup brushes, but then I don't suppose there'll be any great opportunity for that during our period of incarceration at Kamp Kritter. Oh, and Cleo? Don't forget your Blockbuster Video card. I don't have one, as my mommy is too lazy to get out of the house and so uses PPV almost exclusively. I understand *All Dogs Go to Heaven* is out, and though it is surely a fantasy, it might be fun to ridicule. (Anyone knows only cats go to heaven; dogs wander aimlessly in hell, with the heat and the steam and their fur getting all curly and kinky, but that's for another letter.) The sequel to *Homeward Bound* is also out, and while I find it a true stretch of credulity to accept that the cat isn't the one to take the lead and guide those stupid dogs home, I do find that Sassy quite cute. But not as cute as you, dearest Cleo. In fact, you surpass cute. You are elegant, lovely, graceful, and beautiful. Good save, huh?

Okay, okay, okay: so where do we stand? Are we ready? Has the countdown begun? Has your mommy taken out your carriers yet and given them the going-to-the-vet wash-down? Are your travel blankets in the washing machine? Has a stack of canned cat food appeared on the kitchen counter, along with a sack of dry food? Has your mommy tried to track you down, grab your paws, hold you tightly, and trim your claws so you can't make contact with those rude vet techs and draw some real blood? Hm-mmm . . .

Do some detective work, dear Cleo. And as the day approaches when we will again be together, I remain:

Your faithful love,

Tyrone the Tingler

To: TyroneTheGreat@aol.com
From: CleoTheDivine@att.net
Subject: Mouse Mousse, Trout Taupe, and Salmon Sorbet

My Dreamboat, Tyrone,

After reading your last missive about people declawing their cats, I was so upset I simply had to retire to my chaise for a short catnap. Surely, dearest Tyrone, you must be mistaken. Could you have misheard? Unless I am mistaken, a life without claws would preclude manicures, *n'est-ce pas?* Those poor cats would never be able to avail themselves of the many new yummy nail polish colors: Mouse Mousse, Trout Taupe, and Salmon Sorbet. That is so depressing I can't allow myself to think about it for another second for fear of wrinkles.

I know you think you rant, dearest Tyrone, but I choose to look at it as your passionate zest for life. You remind me of Don Quixote. I can see you astride your trusty steed, Roxinante, always on the side of the undercat. That's very noble. I don't particularly fancy Don's armor, however. I would hate to see that gorgeous physique of yours hidden under an aluminum Armani.

The big day is here, and my steamer trunk is packed. It's filled with tons of goodies, including some mouse jerky treats and those chocolate-covered fish balls you like so much. The trunk's a little heavy for me to move. The Big Old Stupid Dog could just nudge it with his big old nose, but so far he's been dogmatic (ha-ha) in his refusal. I must remember to be nice to him occasionally so that he'll do my bidding. On second thought, nah!

I strolled out into the living room, and there was Mommy's Lark luggage and her laptop all stacked neatly for her NY trip. Right next to her stuff was our stuff: freshly washed carriers, and yes, my two favorite little blankets, my catnip red herring, dry cat food, wet cat food, and my running-sore medication.

I know you're fretting that we will be separated at Kamp. But you're forgetting one very important fact, Tyrone. We can charm anyone and get what we want. Just review your bag of tricks. Most people really love it when we gently caress their cheeks with our delicate paws; others are charmed when we crawl inside their briefcase or purse; and who can resist us when we "accidentally" get our heads stuck in a tissue box? Not to worry, my polka-dotted worrywart. We will be together.

Oh-oh. Mommy just called. Said we were going to Kamp. Here I go! Wait a minute! My first inclination is to dash in there and jump into my carrier, but if I did that, Mommy would know something was up. Guess I'll have to hide and let her find me. What I do to give my mommy pleasure.

Just think, *mon cher*, in just a little while, we'll be together. I know all cat carriers look the same, but you won't be able to mistake me in that waiting room. I'll be the only cat wearing a black veil and Gecko Green nail polish—and absolutely nothing else! *Whee!*

Can't wait, can't wait, can't wait,

Your Own Cleo

To: CleoTheDivine@att.net
From: TyroneTheGreat@aol.com
Subject: The Temple of Doom

My Bushel Basket of Wisdom, Cleo,

Following your advice, and upon seeing my very own pet carrier lined up among the others, I decided to hide. All the better to ensure that Mommy wasn't onto our plan, *n'est-ce pas?*

And so, on this very occasion of our soon-to-be tryst, I again hide. I run into the large (read: Mommy's) bathroom. The door is partially closed, so I make myself very sleek and slither in. Ah, quiet and coolness. And a bit of darkness, too, as the light is not on. A most pleasant place, except for that water thing. I mean, drinking out of the toilet is one thing, for it's always fresh and very cool, and easy to reach and splash around in, and I can even understand when Mommy cooks herself, hot dog style, in the large baptismal font, but this make-believe rain from above? Hissing and spitting all spraylike and even a bit hot? I don't think so. Okay, so the hissing and spitting spray is asleep, and I curl up on the fuzzy green rug. Almost like grass, but without that nasty outdoor thing going for it. And then I wake up with a start. It's quiet. Too quiet . . .

I stretch and then clean a paw or two. Even when one is hiding, one must always look one's best. After all, who wants to appear grungy when found? And then I glance at the door. OH MY GOD! The door is closed. Very, very closed. Not even a sliver through which to slither. I lift a mighty paw and pound. Nothing. I meow in my most demanding tone. Then my help-me tone. And then in my most pathetic I'm-trapped-in-here-you-fools tone. Nothing. Oh, no. Do you think they all could have left without me? No. Mommy can count. I've seen her do that with her pathetic penny collection when we're particularly low on chow. How could she have left me? And if she did, why didn't any of my other siblings inform her of her error? They would have, wouldn't they?

Okay, so I just have to wait. I will be rescued. I just must find something with which to amuse myself for the duration. I glance around. Let me see . . .

There's this pink, sort of oval thing on the vanity. Pretty. Sniff, sniff. Smells nice. Lick, lick. *Arghhh!* It tastes like soap! IT *IS* SOAP! What a nasty trick for Mommy to play on me. I hope she doesn't notice the teeth marks. Okay, onward. I stand up on my hind legs and stare at myself in the mirror. So handsome, if I do say so myself. And wait until you see me in my fedora and trench coat! IF you get to see me in my new fedora and trench coat. I'm starting to feel lonely.

Well, there's always the drop-the-bra-into-the-toilet game, but that doesn't last long. I try to flush and the damned thing gets stuck. Water all over the floor. Mommy's fault, of course. If she were not so well endowed, the bra would have been smaller and flushed oh so easily.

Ah, but time is moving slowly. And there's only one thing left: shred the toilet paper. Now, I know, dear Cleo, that you find such trivial pursuits mundane and terribly plebian, but remember I am imprisoned in this temple of cleanliness and must find something to do. And with a full roll on the wooden thing, I begin to play. In fact, I am so engrossed in my minor *divertissement* that I don't hear the knob turn, nor see Mommy looming in the doorway.

"TYRONE!!!"

She can make such a big fuss over practically nothing.

So she scooped me up and hurled me into the office. To wait and contemplate my misdeed, I'm sure. I think she called it a time-out. Whatever.

Any minute now she's going to toss me into my carrier, and we're off to the kennel. I am packed. I am ready. And, personally, if I may be so bold, I just can't wait to sink my teeth into your gentle little neck, hurl you to the ground, and wrestle and play for hours and hours!

Uh-oh, here's Mommy! I'm coming, Cleo. And here I go!

Love,

Tyrone the Trickster

A Few Days Later...

To: CleoTheDivine@att.net
From: TyroneTheGreat@aol.com
Subject: "This Magic Moment . . ."

Dearest Cleo, the Light of My Soul, the Tuna in My Macaroni of Life,

Are you okay? Are you in any trouble? I'm pretty sure my mommy is clueless. At least, I'm mostly pretty sure.

Ah, memories . . .

The trip to the kennel was bumpy and unpleasant, as you can attest. And, once there, I was dumped unceremoniously—still in my carrier—onto the floor of the waiting room. And suddenly, there it was: the undeniable scent of night-blooming jasmine. It could mean only one thing: Cleo was in the building!

Do you recall that moment, Cleo, when our eyes finally met?

Reveal your heart, my little individual-size salmon soufflé and know I miss you already.

Love,

Tyrone the Titan

TO: TyroneTheGreat@aol.com
FROM: CleoTheDivine@att.net
SUBJECT: *An Affair to Remember*

My Precious Pinto, Purveyor of Passion,

The trip home from Kamp Kritter was sad. I was no longer with you, my splotchy hero. Mommy must have sensed my mood because she, too, was uncharacteristically quiet. Or maybe she was having a menopausal moment. Or maybe her trip to New York went poorly. Whatever. She carried me into the house and then dropped me and the dreaded blue carrier on the floor. That's right. Dropped! I bounced across the floor. Hey, lady, this thing doesn't have shock absorbers, you know. She then got down onto the floor and pressed her face right up against the cage. Her voice was very quiet and low when she said she wanted me to think about what I had done for a while. Okay, fine. I thought about our stolen moments together. I thought about the fun we had terrorizing the dogs, especially that wimpy Lhasa apso. I liked the way his hair stood out all over his body, didn't you? I tell you I laughed so hard I almost wet myself. I thought about our romantic evenings: the carp-scented candles, my head in your lap as you read Omar Khayyám's *Rubicat:* "A jug of wine, an eviscerated trout and thou . . ." I thought about stuffing the ferret into that laundry chute. Or maybe it was a mail slot. I thought about the fun we had playing badminton with those liberated "birdies . . ."

I was in the midst of replaying these many wonderful memories when Mommy yanked me out of the cage and started to groom me, brushing me roughly and keeping up a steady diatribe as she went. I tell you that woman carried on like a banshee. (By the way, what exactly is a banshee, anyway? It must be something very unattractive. Something with a very annoying, loud voice.) As Mommy pulled feathers from between my toes, she screamed that because of my antics, you and I have been banned forever from Kamp Kritter. We are never to return. Oh, yeah, that's some terrible punishment, isn't it? We'll never be residents of that koncentration kamp again. Oh, dear, I shall miss the gulag so. Yeah, right. So next time when our mommies go away again, they'll either have to take us along or place us in one of those five-star kitty hostelries.

Everything turned out beautifully, but I will admit I was concerned when I first arrived at Kamp Kritter and you weren't there. I was sitting in my lousy carrier trying to repair a broken nail. There were about a gazillion dogs, barking incessantly. A fair share, too, of scaredy cats who were crying piteously. And a parrot making rude comments (which we won't get into). Suddenly my cage was rudely shaken. I looked up and my entire field of vision was filled with this enormous face. Oh, great, I had a St. Bernard peering in at me. And he was panting. And drooling. Yuck. I would have swatted his big old nose with my delicate little paw, but my nails were still a little tacky, and I'd be damned if I was going to ruin my manicure for a lousy canine. Fortunately, he was suddenly yanked away (thank God for small favors). I

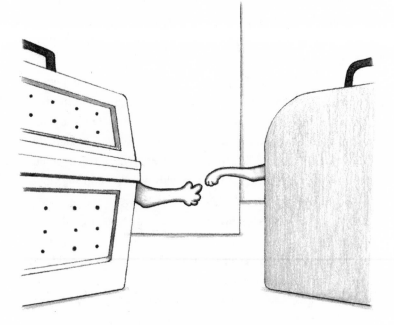

We reached out our delicate paws
through the grates of our respective
prisons and touched . . .
and the music swelled.

glanced out and all I could see was a sea of human and canine legs. In my journal, I try to keep track of Human Truths as I unearth them and I just unearthed a big one. Human Truth #117: People with pale legs and knobby knees should not wear shorts. *Ever.*

I began to panic. What if my beloved Tyrone was already here, but I couldn't see him for all those legs? But surely, I reasoned, I'd be able to pick out his scent. Sniff, sniff. I picked up Wet Dog. Sniff, sniff. A McDonald's Quarter Pounder . . . Some cannabis (naughty, naughty!) . . . Suddenly I heard *clackety, clackety* . . . Actually what I heard was *clackety, clump, clackety, clackety.* I strained my neck to get a better view. There was this kind of flatbed dolly (with one bad wheel) stacked high with carriers. My heart began to race. *Clackety, clump, clackety, clackety.* And now this dolly-thing was right in front of me, and your very own mommy was pulling it. If only that stupid poodle would move . . . and he did. . . . and there you were. Right in front of me in your very own cage. Our eyes met and a cosmic electricity charged the air. We reached out our delicate paws through the grates of our respective prisons and touched . . . and the music swelled.

Everything turned out wonderfully. And then being banned from Kamp Kritter. Could it get any better than that? Although our time together was far too short, I have memories to last for nine lives.

Blushing as I think about our second night together,
Your Very Own Cleo

To: LindaHamner@att.net
From: LVB447@msn.com (L. Virginia Browne)
Subject: A Totally Unnecessary Precaution

Dear Linda,

At first I was, like you, amazed yet nervous. Tyrone and Cleo communicating via e-mail? There was something secretive, even — dare I say it — sinister in the very idea. But, alas, I suspect my fears — and yours — may well have been unfounded.

Our little ones simply wanted to be together, to create a bit of mystery and mischief à deux, and so they did.

While Cleo doesn't appear to be too upset regarding their banishment from Kamp Kritter, I am certain Tyrone is devastated. I can see it in the way he behaves. In fact, I believe completely that his shame over this incident will keep him from ever trying anything like that again.

Trust me: it's out of his system. And, after a time, I'm sure it will be out of Cleo's, too. They wanted to be together, and they were. I'm certain they have no desire to try it again and, if you ask me, I maintain the whole incident was quite traumatizing for them both. They would never, ever undertake such an endeavor again. No, Linda, I am convinced they have learned their lesson.

But, just in case, I might put a block on your Internet provider. Just as a precaution, mind you. A totally unnecessary precaution.

Love,

Virginia

To: LVB447@msn.com (L. Virginia Browne)
From: LindaHamner@att.net
Subject: A Closed Chapter

Dear Virginia,

Yes, yes, I agree. Cleo and Tyrone had their *Excellent Adventure,* and now they seem to be completely over it.

After a prolonged time-out during which I told Cleo to think about her many transgressions at Kamp Kritter, we had a Serious Conversation about her conduct, and she seems to have taken my words to heart. Goodness, she appears completely chastened. She has magically transformed herself into The Perfect Cat. Not once since she's been home has she sat in the middle of my book or harassed the dog or eaten a single plastic bag. I hope her new subdued behavior is the result of her having learned a valuable lesson rather than another bout of constipation.

For some obscure reason, she now spends most of her time in the guest bedroom closet doing God knows what. There's nothing in there but a bunch of old files and office equipment, so there's no way she could get into any trouble. She's probably just thinking about all the heartache she caused at camp. Yes, I'm sure that's it.

I made the office completely off-limits to her, so she no longer has access to the computer. I know it's an unnecessary precaution, but I just didn't want to take any chances. And to tell the truth, she doesn't even seem interested. I'm beginning to wonder if perhaps Cleo and Tyrone had a little kitty spat while they were at camp.

If they continue to be contrite and exhibit good citizenship, perhaps we should arrange a play date for them. Heavily supervised, of course!

Love,

Linda

Diskette III

To: CleoTheDivine@att.net
From: TyroneTheGreat@aol.com
Subject: I've Got a Plan . . .

$\mathcal{D}$ea$\imath e\int \mathcal{C}$leo, the Syrup on My Pancakes, the
Peanut Butter on My Jelly,

When days and days had gone by without a further word from
you, I began to panic. Did I, at Kamp Kritter, commit some incredibly gross faux pas that you found neither clever nor amusing, some ill deed that had—dare I say it?—turned you off? Or,
perish the thought, had your mommy become a complete insom-
niac, which would naturally deny you any computer time at all,
reducing us both to snail mail, although the glue on the backs
of those envelopes is tasty indeed. But no. Happily, joyfully, no.
And that, dear Cleo, is a happy sigh you hear.

From your most recent e-mail, my image of you is thus: you
are sitting in the back of the guest room closet, the newly discovered but fairly old and more than likely forgotten laptop on
your furry tummy, newly programmed and now connected by a
long telephone cord to the Internet and, as a result, e-mail. And
quietly, quietly, you tap away as your mommy conjures images

of you sulking or, perhaps, even sitting shamefully in the closet in disgrace. As if . . .

Well, good news: I, too, have unearthed what I believe to be an identical laptop, also hidden in a bottom file drawer. I suspect these are the ones our mommies took to New York for their last extended visit. Remember how they wailed and shried about how tiny the keyboards were and how little the screens, their fingers clumsily hitting wrong keys and their eyes unable to read? Well, lucky for us we are delicate of paw and keen of sight. These are just right for us!

While I don't have a closet to hide in, I have managed to push the laptop under the king-size bed and then string the telephone cord out from under, behind the nightstand and to the outlet. This should work unless Mommy gets a sudden urge to vacuum under the bed, which probably won't happen until a few weeks or so after the Second Coming.

So, watch out for that cord. Snake it back into the closet when not in use, and I think we'll be okay.

Now, on to new business. I miss you so very much. Our time together at Kamp Kritter lives vividly in my memory as the best time of my life, or lives, as the case may be.

And as for our being banned? Oh, puhleez . . . That place had all the amenities of a puppy mill in Arkansas. Anyway, I do have to play the role of the contrite kitty for a bit, however, just to keep Mommy happy in her assumption that she always knows exactly what I am thinking and feeling. Good heavens, will that woman never stop obsessing about me and leaping to all the wrong conclusions based on her rather simple observations? Why even hope. Besides, she's so terribly easy to lead astray. But this is not the point of my missive. I "missive" [sic] you. So I sat on the newspaper this morning as Mommy was struggling to read

it, and I thought and I thought and I thought. And I think I've come up with an idea.

While at the onerous Kamp Kritter, I overheard some of the dim-witted techies talking of a place where really big and fat rodents roam free, a place completely enclosed—almost a world unto itself—where we could catch and eat our fill and never worry about the supply ending. We could plan another rendez-vous, perhaps on a train or bus.

Have you ever heard of this place? I think it's called Disney-land. . . .

Until we meet again,

And we will!

Your Tyrone

Cleo

Contrary to Cleo's delusions of grandeur, she came from very humble beginnings. Ten years ago (she owns up to six!), Cleo and her twin, Honey, showed up at the Hamners' Sherman Oaks front door, cold, hungry, and looking quite pathetic. Gary and Linda could only keep Honey, so they foisted Cleo onto their friends, who said they'd be by in a couple of days to pick the critter up. Gary and Linda are still waiting.

Cleo moved quickly from gratitude to entitlement to setting up her own fiefdom. Her days consist of eating plastic bags, tossing Mommy's collection of stuffed hedgehogs into the toilet or the Big Old Stupid Dog's water dish, finding new and more diabolical ways to *Gaslight* Mommy and keep in contact with her one true love, Tyrone. This idyllic existence is interrupted only by occasional bouts of constipation.

She is currently at work training the new dog to open cat food cans. And writing a screenplay.

Tyrone

Tyrone is an eight-year-old, seventeen-pound short-haired white cat with black spots so placed as to suggest Zorro, a role played by his namesake, Tyrone Power. Rescued from the local pound with nary a minute to spare, he walked into his new home and immediately assumed the mantle of top cat, a position he holds to this day.

He enjoys corn muffins, taco chips, chocolate-chip cookies, and chocolate milk, which he drinks by dipping his paw into questionably abandoned glasses and licking the purloined treat from his paws. He is very fond of empty boxes and grocery sacks and holds the world's indoor record for both toilet-paper and paper-towel shredding. A somewhat diffident groomer, he allows the female of his family to assume that task, but the feline who holds his heart in her very paws is Cleo, whom he met two years ago and immediately recognized as his soul mate.

Currently, Cleo and Tyrone are deeply involved in a project, the details of which they refuse to reveal to anyone.